D1571037

# TRANSITIONS AND CONSOLIDATION OF DEMOCRACY IN AFRICA

# TRANSITIONS AND CONSOLIDATION OF DEMOCRACY IN AFRICA

Samuel Ebow Quainoo, Ph.D.

Binghamton University, New York
Central State University, Ohio
2008

Library of Congress Cataloging-in-Publication Data

Samuel Ebow Quainoo,
        *Transitions and Consolidation of Democracy in Africa*

ISBN 1-586840-40-1

Published by

Global Academic Publishing
Binghamton University, State University of New York
Binghamton, New York, USA 13902-6000
Phone: (607) 777-4495. Fax: 777-6132
E-mail: gap@binghamton.edu
http://academicpublishing.binghamton.edu

# DEDICATION

To this sweet mother of mine (Nana Akwaaba I) whose love and desire to learn, understand and appreciate different cultures motivated me to become a Comparativist.

# ACKNOWLEDGEMENT

I am indebted to many for their support and encouragement in bringing this book to completion.

I would especially like to express my sincere appreciation for the academic and moral support of Professor Richard Hafferbert, Professor David Cingranelli and Professor Ali A. Mazrui.

Most of all my gratitude goes to my sons Qobi and Qofi whose love sees me through the rigors and joys of life.

# TABLE OF CONTENTS

# LIST OF TABLES

# LIST OF FIGURES

## CHAPTER ONE

# THE DEMOCRATIC RESURGENCE

> The fact that this new nation has succeeded in
> fostering economic growth and democracy under the
> aegis of egalitarian values holds out hope for the rest
> of the world. For prosperity, freedom, and equality
> cannot be for white men only. If they are, then they
> will prove to have been illusory and impermanent as
> the slave-based democracies of ancient Greece (Sey-
> mour Martin Lipset, *The First New Nation: the United
> States in Historical and Comparative Perspective*, 1967,
> p. 395).

## Introduction

What motivates a transition from an authoritarian system to a democracy? How does a transition style affect the
process and result of democratization? Under what conditions
are democracies consolidated in Africa? These questions will be
the main focus of investigation in this book.[1]
The period immediately after 1989 will go down as a wa-
tershed in African political history. Not since the immediate
post-independence period has there been such a dramatic
movement from authoritarian systems towards political plural-
ism (Claude Ake, 1991). Authoritarian regimes in whatever
form have come under a barrage of protests for political reforms and the political landscape of Africa has been altered significantly since then (see David Vick, 1991).
Prior to 1989, the main form of change in government
had been through military coups d'etat, civil wars or at best
political arrangements which transferred power from one auto-
crat to another, usually a crony. By 1985, 38 of the 45 countries of Africa were under autocratic, military or one party rule
(Ake, 1991). Ghana, Nigeria, Benin, Togo, Burkina Faso, Zaire
among others, have all been governed by successive military
juntas.[2] There are others, including Kenya, who have also

managed to transfer power successfully from one personalized ruler to another without the broad masses of the people having any significant involvement in the process.[3]

On the other end, Cote d'Ivoire, Zambia and Tanzania, until quite recently have, for instance, been under one ruler since independence for more than over twenty years. It can be argued that such 'monarchic' tendencies in newly independent states were necessary for political stability because of the turmoil involved in the initial periods of state formation. A multiparty system and its attendant competition was supposed to bring rancor and bitterness, given the deep social cleavages that existed and that continue to exist within many independent Africa.

This pattern of political change and the justification provided by the new African leaders encouraged many political scientists and social analysts to doubt the chances of any form of democratic change in governments on the continent (Samuel P. Huntington, 1993). However, developments after 1989 have shown a trend defying the dominant pattern of political change. There has been a significant movement towards democracy. Curiously enough, this political shift towards democracy has come around without any corresponding improvement in the socio-economic conditions in most countries (see *The Economist*, March 5, 1994, p. 21). Countries that have undergone such changes include Benin, Cape Verde, Congo, Zambia, Madagascar, Malawi and Mali. Incumbent authoritarian regimes have been replaced peacefully with democratically elected ones even though their socio-economic conditions have remained the same or worsened in some cases.[4] Other authoritarian rulers have legitimized their rule by submitting themselves to multi-party elections, and, having won the mandate of the people, transformed their authoritarian systems into democratic ones. Jerry Rawlings of Ghana falls into this category. These positive political changes under the almost stagnant African socio-economic environment, a phenomena defying dominant democratic theory, necessitate fresh evaluation and explanations. There are, however, some authoritarian rulers who are still fighting against the demands of the people for a more democratic political system. President Gnassingbe Eyadema of Togo for instance, is clinging doggedly to the status quo and frustrating all attempts at democratizing the system of governance in his country. There is no doubt that there are still some dark clouds hanging on the democratic horizon but it is an undeniable fact that democracy has broken out in sub-Saharan Africa.

What accounts for these political transformations, however, remains debatable. Dominant democratic theory expects the improvement in the socio-economic conditions to usher in political democracy (see Seymour Martin Lipset, 1959 and 1993). This theoretical expectation of the relationship between economic development and political democracy has not occurred in Africa. The democratic transitions are being motivated by different factors. Even though the style and nature of demands being made by the advocates of democracy and the process of democratization differ from country to country, there seem to be some universal explanations for the simultaneous occurrence of this phenomenon in sub-Saharan Africa. How then does one explain the simultaneity of these protests and demands?

## The Timing of the Demands

The collapse of communism in Eastern Europe and the former Soviet Union, and the peaking of protests and demands for the dismantling of authoritarian political systems in Africa offer some grounds for a theoretical linkage. It can be argued that the political disintegration of the communist bloc orphaned many African autocrats, and made them exceptionally vulnerable to the pro-democracy agitators whose protests have successfully been muffled over the years.

The source of material and moral support for authoritarian regimes in Africa had been sealed with the end of the cold war. This had created enormous logistic problems for some African leaders, in terms of economic handouts to the sycophants in the society who helped prop up the repressive regimes. The collapse of the Soviet empire and the overthrow of authoritarian regimes in its satellite states also eroded any form of moral legitimacy African autocrats had. There were fewer examples of authoritarian government abroad to serve as a point of reference and moral booster for African autocrats. The consequent deprivation of moral support and legitimacy made them more vulnerable to the pressures of the pro-democracy advocates.

The drying up of the source of material support for repressive regimes could be understood better by examining the dynamics of the cold war when it was in operation. Both super powers (the United States and the former Soviet Union) and their African clients benefited from each other. The super powers gleefully provided military and economic resources to strategic African countries to secure their interests, irrespective of the repressive nature of the regime and their human rights record (see Naomi Chazan et al., 1992, pp. 388–410). African authoritarian leaders in turn played the super powers against each other to procure and maintain the flow of the economic and military means to entrench themselves in power. Demands for democracy by the people during the cold war were therefore easily stifled because it was not in the interest of the super powers and the international community stood by unconcerned (see Daniel Pipes, 1991). With the end of the cold war eliminating or reducing considerably the interests outside powers have in Africa, authoritarian regimes have come under more pressure than before, and the only alternative left for them is to acquiesce to the demands of the people for a change in their repressive systems of governance.

The end of the cold war also marked the beginning of externally motivated mounted pressure on African authoritarian leaders to reform their governments. The ever-declining standard of living of the African people, domestic pressure in industrialized countries to trim foreign policy budgets and donor fatigue combined to give African democracy advocates the break they had been waiting for. Good governance has within a short period of time, become pre-requisite for economic and social assistance. The British Foreign Secretary, Douglas Hurd, and the Overseas Development Minister reiterated the change in

British aid policy under which assistance would be denied to countries with non-democratic governments (see *West Africa*, 24 February–1 March, 1992, p. 337). This political conditionality which has now become more of a weapon of the West's foreign policy, has left authoritarian leaders with no viable alternatives but to open the political system up, in order to qualify for the much needed foreign assistance.

African autocrats are now being forced everywhere to admit to the necessity of democratic government to development. Kenya's Daniel Arap Moi for instance, who had consistently defended the institution of a one party system as the only viable political structure for his country because of dreaded potential ethnic conflicts, did a quick turn around and allowed for multi-party elections when aid to the country was suspended. Ghana's Jerry Rawlings, who had hitherto ranted and raved against multi-party democracy as divisive and alien, was forced to call for a national referendum to determine if the majority of the people wanted that form of government. The end of the cold war can therefore be partially credited with hastening the demise of authoritarianism in Africa, even though the process had began long before that event. Specifically, the dramatic increase in the number of protests for democracy in Africa after 1989 could be attributed to the indirect morale boost given to pro-democracy advocates by the collapse of authoritarian regimes in Eastern Europe.

Caution, however, must be exercised not to rely exclusively on external explanations for the political transformations occurring in Africa. There have been many relatively successful struggles for more political participation within and around Africa in recent times. The relative success (albeit at a high cost) and international recognition of the Soweto uprisings in the apartheid South Africa inspired and increased the confidence of pro-democracy advocates.

While it is inaccurate to deny the influence external factors have played in facilitating the movement towards democracy in Africa, it is fair to argue that they only played a secondary role in its explanation. The real impetus for change has been internal and it has been brewing and fermenting for almost a decade.

## Socio-Economic Conditions

Sub-Saharan Africa faced a crisis of confidence in the mid 1980s. There was a feeling of hopelessness brought about by problems from famines, creeping desertification, refugees, human rights violations, coups d'etat, mutually destructive violence, health problems and general economic decline (Sub-Saharan Africa From Crisis to Sustainable Growth, World Bank 1989). These problems, which came to a head around 1975, put enormous pressure on governments on the continent.

Among the economic factors, severe balance of trade deficits caused by weak world commodity prices, fluctuating interest rates which cause national debts to swell to unbearable limits, and a severe drop in international aid and investment combined to create frustratingly high levels of socio-economic hardship. Cost of living skyrocketed as inflation pushed consumer prices through the roof.

Africa's image abroad as reported in the international media heightened tensions already existing between the rulers and the ruled. The seed of distrust that had been sown between the rulers and the ruled continued to blossom, in spite of gradual economic improvements in the early 1980s.

External aid to Africa increased significantly after much sympathy had been generated in international circles because of the previous years' socio-economic disaster. In addition to the increase in aid, prices of raw materials (the backbone of most African economies) began to rise again, boosting Africa's foreign exchange earnings. The absence of rainfall, which hitherto had been a major problem to farmers, came down during this period to mitigate the effects of the severe drought and farming. The net result of all these positive economic factors is that consumer prices in Africa (as reported in the International Monetary Fund's Statistical Yearbook 1970–90) came tumbling down dramatically.[5] Surprisingly, the gradual rise of the cost of living after its sharp decline (see figure 1.1) met with protests for political reforms. Figure 1.1 illustrates the pattern of socio-economic hardships between 1970 and 1990. What theoretical explanation accounts for these seemingly contradictory pheomena?

## Figure 1.1
## CONSUMER PRICE TRENDS IN
## 'PROTEST' COUNTRIES

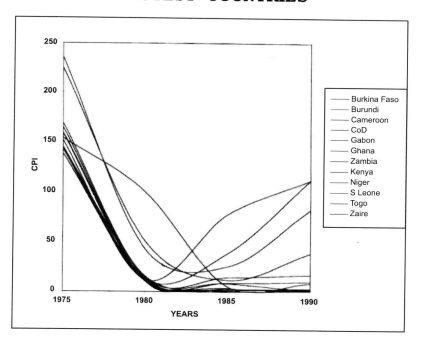

Source: IMF Statistics, 1970, 1980, 1990

## Table 1.1
### *Protests for Democracy Since 1989*

| COUNTRY | DATE FOR ELECTIONS |
|---|---|
| Benin | 1991 |
| Burkina | 1991 |
| Cameroon | 1991 |
| Cape Verde | 1991 |
| Comoros | 1990 |
| Congo | 1992 |
| Cote d'Ivoire | 1990 |
| Gabon | 1990 |
| Guinea-Bissau | 1993 |
| Ghana | 1992 |
| Kenya | 1992 |
| Madagascar | 1996 |
| Malawi | 1994 |
| Mali | 1992 |
| Sao Tome | 1990 |
| South Africa | 1994 |
| Tanzania | 1995 |
| Zambia | 1991 |

Sources: Arthur Banks' *Political Handbook of the World*, 1995, and Michael Bratton and Nicolas van de Walle, 1992

## Theoretical Underpinnings

Why did the protests and demand for democracy fail to occur in 1975, the peak of the socio-economic hardships? Why was there a record number of protests between 1986 and 1989, a period that comparatively witnessed a better set of economic conditions than the 1975 period where there were worse conditions? By the end of 1988, either the people or the elite in countries including Benin, Burkina Faso, Cameroon, Cape Verde, Ghana, Mali, Zambia and Zaire had all tabled strong demands for some form of change leading towards democratization of their political systems of one form or another (see table 1.1 for a list of protests in Africa during the period under description). The democracy movement on the continent took off at this point. A theoretical explanation of the simultaneity of events is needed at this juncture.

James C. Davies' (1962) theory of revolution becomes very pertinent in explaining the post-1986 political events on the continent. According to him, people who have long endured harsh Conditions would not tolerate them anymore even in a relatively reduced form, after they had experienced a short form of reprieve from those conditions. The break in their suffering creates an expectation unimagined before. A new belief that things need not be bad after all is fostered. This new glimpse of hope therefore reduces the previous levels of tolerance for hardships or suffering.

The 1980 reprieve in Africa's socio-economic hardship provided the people with the motivation and the fillip to demand more participation in government and a political system that is more accountable and transparent. Davies contends that:

> Revolutions are most likely to occur when a prolonged period of objective economic and social development is followed by a short period of sharp reversal. People then subjectively fear that grounds gained with great effort will be quite lost; their mood becomes revolutionary.

After the sharp socio-economic improvement in 1986, a small but consistent decline began to set in gradually. The confidence level of African authoritarian leaders at this point began to decline with the rising gloomy socio-economic hardships. In addition to the doubts raised about the quality of leadership, the perception of the people about social and political institutions changed. The capabilities of the rulers and the institutions under which they have been misruled became the focus of protestors.

Long neglect and abuse of political institutions that was not accountable had produced a lot of waste and decay. It is not surprising that the people lost confidence in almost all of the national institutions including the administrative, educational and judiciary machinery of government. For instance, the 1987 World Bank sponsored study on Africa titled, *Sub-Sahara Africa From Crisis To Sustainable Growth,* p. 22, had this to say:

> ... This widespread institutional decay is symbolized by the poor physical condition of once world-class institutions such as The University of Legon in Ghana and Makerere University in Uganda, by the breakdown of Judicial systems in a number of countries, by the poor state of once high-quality roads, and by the dilapidation of once well-functioning railways.

Authoritarian rule had at this point began to lose any semblance of credibility. The legitimacy of rulers as well as most of the institutions, under which the oppressive and wasteful misrule had been conducted, came under constant scrutiny, hence the demand for the overhauling of the whole political system.

By 1989 therefore, when the communist edifice in Eastern Europe and the former Soviet Union came tumbling down, authoritarian regimes could no longer contain the bottled-up feelings and the demands for more democratic systems of governance. All of the corrupt rulers who relied on the Eastern bloc, including those that had been favored by the West (for self-interest reasons), could not escape the onslaught of the pro-democracy protests because they had both lost the moral authority and the material support to contain the challenge to their continued misrule. The corrupt and authoritarian leaders who relied on the Communist regimes lost a valuable form of support when the cold war ended.

## Conclusion

Understanding political developments in one country is difficult enough; explaining continental political phenomena can be extremely hazardous because of the specificities of individual country cases. And yet, there are common denominators in all of the cases, which provide a basis for careful generalizations.

At this point, it suffices to argue that both regional and international events impacted greatly the advocation for democratic forms of government in Africa around the latter part of 1989. These events, however, only reinforced domestic pressure for the same purpose; a pressure that had been mounted over quite a period of time but denied any success because of the intransigence of African autocrats and the support they received by playing the super powers against each other for their own self-interests. Once the strategic importance of Africa diminished as a result of the end of the cold war, advocates of democracy in individual countries could no longer be denied, hence the simultaneity of the current political events.

## An Outline of the Dissertation

The dissertation focuses on conditions, style and processes of the transitions from authoritarian rule to forms of democracy. It hypothesizes that democratic transitions are initiated by socio-economic hardships. It also argues that transition styles, which are influenced by socio-political and hisorical factors, have major impact on the form of democracy a country ends up with. It may even affect the chances of consolidation of the democratic gains.

Africa has undergone a similar major political transformation in the immediate past. The decolonization exercise that peaked around 1960 transformed the political landscape of Africa, with many newly independent countries drafting democratic constitutions as the basis of their newly formed governments. But things went wrong shortly after that when victorious political leaders and elites failed to adhere to the dictates of the constitutions. Political power became an end in itself, and constitutions were either gradually tampered with, or violent take-overs became the norm for changing governments.

The need for a search for the linchpins of democratic consolidation has therefore assumed new urgency, to avoid the backsliding that was experienced after the 'first democratic liberation' in the 1960s. The dissertation also examines, and analyzes critically, the variables behind the success of African democracies. For instance, if lack of socio-economic development initiates a movement towards democracy, will the same variable be a sufficient condition for democratic consolidation?

The earlier chapters take a cross-national approach, examining the validity of often cited relevant variables that are necessary for democratic transition and consolidation.[6] The latter chapters focus on individual countries, selecting a case each to represent transitional and consolidating patterns. The study also probes for factors responsible for that democratic consolidation. Finally, an African democratization model is derived relying on the insights gained from the case studies.

## Notes to Chapter One

1.  The dissertation specifically examines two types of transitions, the bottom-up and top-down approaches. It also investigates the conditions that facilitate democracy in Africa.

2.  The figures given here are of 1993 only. The frequency at which African countries alternate between types of governments (military, civilian, single-party and multi-party systems) has been high. For an up-date, see current issues of *African Demos*, a publication of Emory University, Atlanta.

3.  Jomo Kenyatta, founder and first President of Kenya, was succeeded by his protege, Daniel arap Moi. Such arrangements are quite common in Africa.

4.  In all these countries, there have been on-going battles for change of governments. Success in Benin, the first transition to democracy, probably convinced the others that it is not a fight in futility.

5.   African countries are most vulnerable to the wrangling of the international market because of their dependence on single commodities as the backbone of the economy.

6.   The study selects factors that have been cited specifically in relation to Africa. They include development, ethnicity, religion and colonial heritage.

## Questions to Chapter One

1. What are the main motivations to the democratic transitions in Africa in the 1990s?

2. What is theory of Revolution? Who proposed it? Explain its significance with respect to the political events in Africa after 1986?

## CHAPTER TWO
# THE DEMOCRACY DEBATE

## Introduction

Democracy as a system of government has become more attractive to developing countries because it is believed to offer a better platform for all to participate in the development effort, but more importantly, it provides a broader forum for representation in the distribution of national resources (Larry Diamond, 1988). While the merits for this belief are discussed fully in chapter seven, it is fair to argue that the desirability of democracy to developing countries increased after the end of the cold war because of the notion that Western democracy has triumphed over communism (Francis Fukuyama, 1989).

Much has been written and continues to be written on what democracy is, what it offers, and the conditions under which it is attained and sustained.[1] From Aristotle to Zolberg, different conceptions and definitions of democracy have been given, some overlapping with each other, while others differ in certain significant aspects (see for instance, Robert Alan Dahl, 1986; Hans-Dieter Kingemann and Richard I. Hofferbert, 1994). Differences in conceptualization have arisen mainly because of the diversity of the societies in which democracy as a political system has been practiced. Before one settles on a definition of democracy, there needs to be a brief survey of some of the relevant conceptualizations that have been advanced in the social sciences. This effort will provide the background to our understanding of the political developments taking place in Africa.

## Conceptualizations

Democracy is elusive both as a concept and as an objective. In spite of the contention that democracy as it is now practiced traces its ancestry to Ancient Greece, there is an embarrassingly high number of conceptualizations among social scientists. Some of them are based on ideology while others depend on one's social orientation. For instance, both Marxist-biased scholars and non-Marxist sympathizers have laid claim to higher levels of democracy in their opposing political systems (see for example, Barry Clark, 1991). Some third world scholars who are culturally sensitive to their traditional authority systems, have also disagreed with the characterization of their systems as undemocratic, objecting to the use of first world indicators as measuring yardsticks (see Julius K. Nyerere 1968).

Democracy has been conceptualized and defined in both normative and empirical senses. Peter Bachrach's (1980) definition for instance, borders on the normative because of its idealist expectations. He sees democracy as a system of government that allows for the maximization of the self-development of the individual. Robert Dahl's definition followed in a similar tradition when he characterized democracy as a system of government that is completely responsible to its citizens. While such definitions provide a solid philosophical ground for conceptualizing democracy, it offers little in terms of measurement for empirical comparisons of different societies.[2] The abstract nature of such definitions make it difficult to ascertain the performance of the political system, especially for comparative purposes. There are however, some scholars whose definitions circumvent such problems because they adopt an institutional, rather than an idealistic approach.

J. A. Schumpeter (1947) describes a democratic system as one that allows its important decision makers to be elected periodically. The competition for such positions should be freely organized and all adults should have the opportunity to compete for the decision-making positions as well as the chance to elect representatives of their choice. Lipset (1959, p. 27) echoes similar sentiments because of the institutional bias of his definition:

> Democracy in a complex society may be defined as a
> political system which supplies regular constitutional
> opportunities for changing government officials, and

as a social mechanism which permits the largest possible part of the population to influence major decisions by choosing among contenders for political office.[3]

In spite of the differences among many of the definitions, the underlying principles of competitiveness, representation and participation in an atmosphere of freedom and fairness are the same. These common strands still connect the
normative and the empirical definitions. The democratic ideal
which according to the Ancient Greeks and modern day Utili-
tarians is to "... enable individuals or identified groups to exercise their rights and protect their interests as active participants in the political arena" (C. H. Dodd 1979, p. 176), has
continued to remain the cornerstone of all political systems
that aspire to democracy. Different institutions informed by
different historical processes, however, have been created to
achieve this democratic objective, springing up different forms
of democracy. In the industrialized world for instance, both
Sweden and the United States of America are considered societies with consolidated democratic systems (Raymond Gastil,
1994).[4] And yet there are differences between the two in terms
of the role of government, the number of political parties, and
the type of institutions performing the same or similar functions.

## Forms of Democracy

In Africa, Robert Pinkley's (1994) topology of democracies provides a good instruction. His categorization which covers broadly the views of the leading scholars on the field, iden-
tifies five main types of democracy: Radical, Guided, Liberal,
Socialist, and Consociational democracies. This categorization
by no means presupposes that elements in each democracy
type are exclusive to that type. There are overlapping in-
stances, in spite of their broad differing features. A democracy,
for instance, may be both liberal and consociational at the
same time, as perhaps exists in Mauritius.

*Radical democracy.* This form of democracy is perhaps the closest to the version of Ancient Greece. Individuals are expected to participate fully in politics to exercise their rights and to protest their interests. Decisions are taken based on a crude majoritarian basis. The complexity of modern day societies has rendered this version almost unpracticable. Under radical democracy, society is seen as an aggregation of individuals, and no regard is given to the existence of groups of any sort. In contemporary societies however, ethnicity, religion, class, gender and race among other social divisions, have increasingly become a point of identification and have gained constituencies of their own. It has become almost impossible for a democratically-elected government not to cater to the interests of these powerful groups and still remain in power. Needless to say, a democracy based on a simple majority has the tendency of neglecting the needs and aspirations of the minority. In Africa, where the political landscaping has produced an intriguing composition of ethnic groupings in countries, radical democracy (which ignores the interests of ethnic or cultural minorities) has been problematic. It has contributed to the taking over of democratic polities by authoritarian rulers, who have in the end pretentiously justified their rule by pointing to the insensitivity of multi-party politics. For instance, the "northerners" in Nigeria have always been voted into power when simple majoritarian electoral means have been used to select political leaders, creating discontent among the "southerners," who finally overthrow constitutionally-elected governments under that pretence. Radical democracies have therefore not lasted long in societies where they have been practiced, especially in Africa.

*Guided Democracy.* This form of democracy differs from radical democracy in that it regards society as a whole with common goals and interests. Individual interests and rights are protected as long as they conform to that of the national interest as perceived by the elected rulers. In these democracies, the attainment of the *general will* (as espoused by Rousseau) is paramount and it is the sole duty of the state to see to its achievement. Political leaders are elected as in any democracy, but since they decide what the common interests of the people are, they sooner than later use whatever means possible to force their wishes on the majority. An elite ruling class is created which uses fair and unfair means to perpetuate itself in power. Gambia under Dauda Jawara is an example of this form of democracy.

Some African leaders have found guided democracy, at its worst, very convenient. Zambia under Kaunda before it degenerated into the authoritarian mode, experienced the guided form of democracy. Elections were conducted alright, but it was the leader who decided what the national agenda was. If in doing so, the rights and interests of individuals, groups, or even the majority were trampled upon, so be it.

Under this form of democracy, members of the society are allowed to participate in politics but the issues to be debated are solely decided by the national leader. Many leaders manage to get away with this system which borders on authoritarianism because they moralize and rationalize undemocratic practices by invoking the fear of the consequences of unnecessary disagreements along ethnic or religious lines. Under President Moi (in spite of the recent elections), Kenya can still be considered as an example of a guided democracy, albeit in its worst form.

Guided democracy and radical democracy, as different as they may be, regarding the protection of rights of individuals, provide the majority and the state as a whole with one thing in common; they are very close to authoritarianism. Under both forms, the people do not have much say in the issues discussed, and also the interests of significant minorities are usually trampled upon. Leaders may be selected through fair elections but the interests of citizens are for most part ignored.

*Liberal Democracy.* Liberal democracy is what normally pertains in most western industrialized societies. This form of democracy recognizes the rights and interests of both individuals and groups in a modern society of complex social interests. A form of representation is therefore adopted to address the diversity of interests. Admitting that society is made up of diverse groups with different interests, the state provides the platform for the competition that naturally ensues. Ideally, the state is to referee the competition in a manner that ensures that individual and minority rights are not sacrificed for the majority, in the free-for-all competition.

In Africa, Mauritius is perhaps the closest example of this form of democracy. Its unique historical origins may have influenced the choice of its form of democracy. Being a former colony of both Britain and France, and having experienced a forced importation of massive labor from the African mainland and Asia, Mauritian society is highly diverse along ethnic, religious, linguistic and class lines. This diversity has encouraged a parliamentary system where minority interests are catered for constitutionally and in practice through the concept of coalitions.

Liberal democracy is not without flaws. The focus on liberties and freedom can sometimes create moral problems. In a world where extreme inequalities (social and economic) exist, it is almost impossible to create a level playing field for free competition. Historical circumstances have given some groups a better start and created deep inequalities, and the wealthier sections of the society (who usually happen also to be the legislators), may naturally be tempted to maintain the status quo. These criticisms of liberal democracy have been advanced by many African leaders who have rejected the Western-styled multi-party system. Jerry Rawlings, during his authoritarian days in Ghana, used this line of argument to justify his overthrow of a liberal democracy under Hilla Limann. The conversion of Jerry Rawlings in the 1990s (now a champion of liberal democracy), has further discredited authoritarian styles of government in Africa; especially since the socio-economic conditions in the country have taken a dramatic upswing in the last few years.

Liberal democracy has capitalism as its twin. Empirically, this form of democracy has proved to be the most economically productive and therefore most attractive to African countries with shattered economies.[5] However, the case exists that liberal democracy must not only set guidelines or rules to regulate political competition, but must also ensure social and economic equality to make it more workable in Africa.

    *Socialist democracy.* This form of democracy, whose advocates believe it to be at a higher level than liberal democracy, places emphasis on equality and social justice. It shares its perception of society as an organic entity of common interests with the proponents of guided democracy. It, however, differs from guided democracy in the sense that socialist democracy believes society has to be transformed first by the state. It is bound to protect citizens' rights and interests, unless doing so comes into conflict with the pursuit of equality and justice. It also calls for vigorous re-distributive policies and a collective ownership of the means of production. This form of democracy may be on a higher plane of idealism than the other forms. Most of its ideals have, however, proved to be impossible to attain in practice.

    Tanzania under Julius Nyerere is a classic example. Through its Ujamaa system, Nyerere tried to create a society where means of production would be nationally or at least communally owned (Nyerere, 1968). The problem with the Tanzanian system, as with most other socialist democracies, is that efficient means of production should be in place first to create what has to be distributed later on. In Tanzania, where the state produced so little, not much distribution could be done.

    Ghana, under Kwame Nkrumah is another example, even though it tried to circumvent the problem Tanzania faced. Nkrumah sacrificed certain aspects of the socialist democracy ideals to create a resource base for redistribution. For instance, unlike Nyerere, Nkrumah openly courted foreign multi-national companies to operate in Ghana to help generate the needed funds for his social programs. The problem with such an approach is the difficulty in attracting highly profit-motivated capitalist companies to operate in an environment where there is a high potential for nationalization of private companies.

    Nkrumah has been criticized sometimes for creating an extraordinarily attractive investment climate for foreign companies. For instance, Ali Mazrui (1986) has argued that

Nkrumah's deal with Kaiser Engineers of America for the construction of the Akosombo Dam and the Valco smelting plant set Ghana's development back for decades because he was taken advantage of by the powerful multi-national corporation.[6] This form of democracy has run into problems because it has failed to produce what it wants to distribute; it may require individual motivation and economic efficiency which is hard to attain under the dictates of socialist democracy.

*Consociational Democracy.* Consociational democracy may be the answer to the weaknesses of radical democracy. While the latter freezes out the rights and interest of the minorities for the sake of the majority, the former ensures a full participation of minorities by either reserving a specific number of seats for them in the government, or by a carefully crafted form of proportional representation. Proponents of this form of democracy (David Apter 1961, Arend Lijphart 1977) argue that it creates consensus and loyalty among all groups in society, giving the government a high degree of legitimacy. The state acts as a negotiator in inter-group conflicts, ensuring stability and peace in the political process. Citizens' rights and interests are protected either directly by the state or through the powers of the recognized groups.

The Republic of South Africa has started on the path of this form of democracy. In order to ensure the continued stay of whites who own the capital in the republic when it became black- ruled, a system was created to give them a voice in government disproportionate to their total numerical strength in the electorate. Other black ethnic groups who are significantly out-numbered have also been given ample representation in the government because of their specific position in the country's political history; thus Chief Buthelezi in spite of his sounding defeat enjoys an important position in government because he represents the majority of the Zulus and their Nkatha movement. Ethiopia offers a classic example of consociational democracy. To avoid the tensions or wars generated by ethnic conflicts, it has introduced a strong federal system, dividing the country into ethnically based regions (*The Chris-*

*tian Science Monitor,* April 23, 1996). The idea is to provide easier access to all ethnic groups in the business of government.

There are problems associated with consociational democracy as well. An attempt to give minorities a voice can easily degenerate into a dictatorship by the minority. A constant use of the veto power by the minority can create too many stalemates, making the business of governing impossible. It can also be argued that denying the "one person, one vote" principle can be interpreted as playing favoritism to powerful interests in society. Such a system can also perpetuate existing cleavages in society. There are still some hurt feelings in South Africa, especially among some radical leaders of the African National Congress (ANC) who believe that the Mandela government kowtowed to the white minority with regard to the retention of political power by the former apartheid practitioners, even under black majority rule.

The above discussion about democracy demonstrates that there are elements of democracy in most political systems and those characterized as democratic come in many different forms and variations. It is therefore fair to assume that even among democracies, one can be more democratic than the other. There are different degrees of democracy. It becomes authoritarian when it loses all the degrees of democracy. How then, can democracy be measured and compared?

## Measurement of Democracy

Measuring democracy has attracted as much scholarly attention and debate as the definition of the concept. From Arthur Banks (1976) democracy scores to Raymond Gastil's annual state of the world freedom measurements, social scientists have strived to improve the accuracy and reduce the biases in such exercises as much as possible.

Kenneth Bollen (1980) and Robert W. Jackman (1985) for instance, have been involved in this exercise. They measure the performance of the institutions of democracy by examining among others, the fairness of elections, methods of selection for both the executive and the legislation, and the freedom of the press.

The political data from the annual report on the state of freedom around the world is one of the most reliable sources. Sirow and Inkeles (ct. in Lipset 1993) confirm this claim when they tested measures of democracy including Gastil's, and found a 0.75 average coefficient of determination of the inter-correlations. The high level of inter-correlation suggest a fair amount of agreement among the various measurements of institutional democracy. Gastil's data set which measures a composite score of political and civil liberties is utilized in this study because, in addition to its consistency, it includes almost all African countries and also covers all the years under this study.[7]

The next logical step in this study after settling on a method of measurement of political democracy, is to identify the type of conditions that have sustained democracy in Africa. The recent democratic gains have been made without a corresponding improvement in the economic well-being of the people. Is economic development a necessary or sufficient condition for democracy? How much of Africa's cultural heterogeneity is a hindrance to democratic consolidation? The next chapter focuses on the conditions that have facilitated democracy in Africa.

## Notes to Chapter Two

1.     See for example, Diamond et al. (1988).

2.     Huntington (1984) for instance, criticizes the usefulness of such definitions for comparative purposes.

3.     Lipset 1959 definition is also cited by Pourgerami (1991, p. 3).

4.     Raymond Gastil's measurement which goes back to 1972 has consistently listed both the United States of America and Sweden as having consolidated democracies.

5.       The merits of democracy, especially its capacity for economic development and conflict resolution are fully discussed in chapter seven.

6.       Mazrui's assertion is made in volume four of his televised series on Africa (1986). This particular comment is under the 'Tools of Exploitation' title.

7.       Gastil derived his composite score by measuring the extent of political rights and civil liberties of countries. Political rights include free and fair elections, competitive political groupings, genuine opposition roles, and self-determination for minority groups. Civil liberties consist of freedoms of expression, assembly and demonstration, religion and association. They include also, protection of the individual from political violence, harm from the courts and security forces. Countries are rated from 1–7, with one being the country with the highest of these ideals and 7 being the worst. The average score of political rights and civil liberties determines a country's overall freedom rating. Freedom ratings are appropriated as democracy scores in this study because they measure the same elements of a democratic government. For the purposes of clarity and clearer illustration, the study inverts Gastil's scores where 7 describes the presence of the highest degree of democracy in a country, with 1 being the lowest.

## Questions to Chapter Two

1. What is the democratic ideal?

2. Explain in detail the different forms of Democracy.

# CHAPTER THREE
# CONDITIONS FOR DEMOCRACY

## Introduction

Democracy does not come naturally to any society. Throughout history, men and women have tried to rule others without having to be elected or accountable in the fashion that democratic societies demand today. From Kings and Chiefs, through religious leaders and military men and women, every society in one form or the other has been subjected to un-democratic rule in some period of its history. But some societies have been able to move away from these forced rules and establish democracies while others have not, prompting the search for the conditions that have helped those successful cases.

It must be borne in mind that determining conditions in which democracies have been instituted does not necessarily establish a cause and effect relationship. The exact causal relationship of these conditions on democracies may be difficult to determine, given the plethora of variables that may have some influence on the system. But the consistent association of certain variables with democracy in different societies should be indicative of the significance of that condition to democracy. The recent democratization wave on the continent gives cause for a search for democratic conditions (table 3.1 provides democratic gains made between 1980 and 1990).

# Table 3.1
## *Changes in Democracy Scores in Africa, 1980–1990*

| COUNTRY | 1980 | 1990 | CHANGE |
|---|---|---|---|
| Angola | 1.0 | 2.0 | 1.0 |
| Benin | 1.5 | 5.5 | 4.0 |
| Botswana | 5.5 | 6.5 | 1.0 |
| Burkina Faso | 2.5 | 3.0 | 0.5 |
| Burundi | 2.0 | 2.5 | 0.5 |
| C. Africa Rep. | 2.0 | 2.5 | 0.5 |
| Cameroon | 2.0 | 2.5 | 0.5 |
| Chad | 1.5 | 2.0 | 0.5 |
| Congo | 3.5 | 5.0 | 1.5 |
| Ethiopia | 1.0 | 3.0 | 2.0 |
| Gabon | 2.0 | 4.0 | 2.0 |
| Gambia | 5.0 | 6.5 | 1.5 |
| Ghana | 2.5 | 3.0 | 0.5 |
| Guinea | 1.0 | 2.5 | 1.5 |
| Kenya | 3.0 | 3.5 | 0.5 |
| Lesotho | 3.0 | 3.0 | 0 |
| Liberia | 2.0 | 1.5 | -.5 |
| Madagascar | 3.0 | 4.0 | 1.0 |
| Malawi | 1.5 | 1.5 | 0 |
| Mali | 1.5 | 5.5 | 4.0 |
| Mauritius | 6.0 | 6.0 | 0 |
| Mozambique | 1.0 | 3.0 | 2.0 |
| Niger | 1.5 | 3.0 | 1.5 |
| Nigeria | 5.5 | 3.5 | -2.0 |
| Rwanda | 2.0 | 3.0 | 1.0 |
| Senegal | 4.0 | 4.5 | 0.5 |
| Sierra Leone | 3.0 | 1.5 | -1.5 |
| Somalia | 1.0 | 1.0 | 0 |
| Togo | 1.5 | 2.5 | 1.0 |
| Uganda | 3.0 | 2.5 | -.5 |
| Zaire | 1.5 | 2.5 | 1.0 |
| Zambia | 2.5 | 5.5 | 2.5 |
| Zimbabwe | 4.0 | 3.5 | -.5 |
| TOTAL | 83.5 | 111.5 | 28.0 |
| Average | 2.5 | 3.3 | .84 |

Source: Raymond Gastil (1980, 1990).

This chapter will examine the relationship of the variables that have often been cited to be either negatively or positively associated with democracy in Africa. They include development, ethnicity, religion, and colonial heritage.

## Democratic Conditions

*Development.* For decades, there has been an ongoing debate about the relationship between democracy and socio-economic development. Alex Inkeles et al. (1990) evaluate comprehensively other studies that look at the correlation between political regime-type and economic development.

One side of the debate argues in favor of the potential of economic development inducing political democracy because of the compatibility of the two (see Lipset 1959, 1993, 1994; Diamond 1988). The opposing view postulates that political democracy is a ** hindrance to economic development because it unduly raises expectation (especially in the developing countries) which cannot be met in the short run, and therefore ends up creating political instability which is inimical to development. Apter (1965), for instance, contends that authoritarianism is the most appropriate system for such societies because it offers a better means of overcoming conflicts that arise out of social heterogeneity.

Lipset (1959), in particular, finds a strong correlation between economic development and democracy. Lipset's general conclusion confirms economic development as the main driving force for democratic development. This finding reinforces the empirical picture of almost all economically developed countries enjoying political systems with high degrees of democracy. It supports the view that it is not sheer coincidence that the group of seven (who are all economically developed) also have societies with the highest degrees of democracy.

Convincing as Lipset's findings about socio-economic pre-requisites of democracy may seem, a significant number of scholars have questioned the logic behind extrapolating such a relationship to all societies, because it flies in the face of empirical evidence (see for example, Dunkwart Rustow 1970). For instance, the exceptional economic growth of Latin American countries in the 1960s and 1970s did not move its political systems toward democracy, as Lipset's finding would expect.

Such examples have prompted other scholars including Terry Lynn Karl (1991) to question the relationship between democracy and economic development. Analyzing the recent democratic transitions in Latin America, Karl postulates that socio-economic conditions may better be treated as products of consolidated democracies rather than as pre-requisites of their existence.

African countries have perennially clustered at the bottom of both economic development and democracy scales (see Phillips Cutright 1965). While Ziyad Limam (1991), for instance, agrees that lack of economic development is hazardous to democracy in Africa as elsewhere in the world, John Healey (1992) contends that no significant relationship exists between regime type and economic development in Africa.

Dirk Berg-Schlosser (1984) has also concluded that it is political stability and not a specific regime-type, that correlates with economic development. The debate becomes even more confusing when it is ascertained that both authoritarian systems and democracies are capable of creating political stabilities, hence the need for further examination of the relationship between development and democracy.

*Measuring Development.* Finding indicators that measure development accurately is difficult. Measuring development in Africa is extremely problematic for a number of reasons. Record keeping of governmental activities has relatively not been of the best quality in Africa, either because of lack of resources or for sheer political reasons. Again, far too many African economic activities take place in the informal sector, rendering indicators which measure formal activities such as the Gross Domestic Product (GDP) and the Gross National Income (GNI) quite unreliable. There is also the problem of over-generalization, which normally characterizes studies of global proportion.

The economic wealth of Africa as a region measured in GDP, is on the average so much lower than the rest of the world to the extent that research of such nature that groups all countries of the world together misses the dynamics of regional patterns. Analyzing African countries exclusively can therefore unmask significant developments that are easily played down or lost in a global study. Problems of data availability and reliability have, however, limited such a strong area focus. Of thirteen studies on democracy and economic performance, only Berg Schlossers' was based on Africa alone (Healey and Robinson 1992, p. 110).

The study utilizes the Human Development Index (HDI) data compiled by the United Nations Development Program (UNDP) because its definition of development is much broader.[1] The broader scope of the HDI measurement of development captures more activities that contribute to development, unlike other measurements such as the GDP and the GNI that focus only on economic activities.[2]

Utilizing the HDI and Gastil/Freedom House data, it is observed that a strong relationship exists between development and democracy globally. Generally, most countries with high HDI also have high scores on the democracy scale as illustrated on figure 3.1.[3] This finding is compatible with the findings of most of the studies including those of Lipset, Cutright, and Diamond, with a democracy-development correlation of 0.64. Surprisingly, in 1990 when democracy scores generally increased in Africa, HDI scores decreased (see table 3.2 for the degree of increase in democracy scores and the corresponding decrease in the Human Development scores between 1980 and 1990). Within the ten year period, the correlation between democracy and development weakened from 0.44 in 1980 to 0.33 in 1990 (see appendix). This curious relationship refutes the conclusions reached by scholars that development induces democracy. What factors then, influence democracy in Africa?

## Table 3.2
### *Changes in Human Development Index and Democracy*

| COUNTRY | HDI 1980 | HDI 1990 | HDI CHANGE | DEM. 1980–1990 |
|---|---|---|---|---|
| Angola | .48 | .15 | -.33 | 1.0 |
| Benin | .19 | .11 | -.08 | 4.0 |
| Botswana | .42 | .52 | .10 | 1.0 |
| Burkina Faso | .12 | .08 | -.04 | 0.5 |
| Burundi | .19 | .17 | -.02 | 0.5 |
| C. Africa Rep. | .22 | .16 | -.06 | 0.5 |
| Cameroon | .35 | .32 | -.03 | 0.5 |
| Chad | .12 | .08 | -.04 | 0.5 |
| Congo | .34 | .37 | .03 | 1.5 |
| Ethiopia | .10 | .16 | .06 | 2.0 |
| Gabon | .47 | .51 | .04 | 2.0 |
| Gambia | .13 | .06 | -.07 | 1.5 |
| Ghana | .32 | .31 | -.01 | 0.5 |
| Guinea | .12 | .06 | -.06 | 1.5 |
| Kenya | .38 | .39 | .01 | 0.5 |
| Lesotho | .34 | .49 | .25 | 0 |
| Liberia | .28 | .43 | .15 | -.5 |
| Madagascar | .24 | .37 | .13 | 1.0 |
| Malawi | .18 | .17 | -.01 | 0 |
| Mali | .11 | .07 | -.04 | 4.0 |
| Mauritius | .64 | .83 | .19 | 0 |
| Mozambique | .21 | .15 | -.06 | 2.0 |
| Niger | .10 | .07 | -.03 | 2.0 |
| Nigeria | .32 | .24 | -.08 | -2.0 |
| Rwanda | .28 | .21 | -.07 | 1.0 |
| Senegal | .17 | .18 | .01 | 0.5 |
| Sierra Leone | .10 | .04 | -.06 | -1.5 |
| Somalia | .25 | .11 | -.14 | 0 |
| Togo | .23 | .22 | -.01 | 1.0 |
| Uganda | .31 | .20 | -.11 | -.5 |
| Zaire | .33 | .29 | -.04 | 1.0 |
| Zambia | .37 | .35 | -.02 | 2.5 |
| Zimbabwe | .49 | .41 | -.08 | -.5 |
| TOTAL | 8.9 | 8.3 | -0.6 | 28.0 |
| AVERAGE | .26 | .25 | -.01 | .84 |

Source: United Nations Development Program and R. Gastil.

In 1980 only a few African countries had any appreciable score on the democracy scale. A decade later (1990), while
the group of seven still retains their 1980 positions, there had
been significant improvement in the scores of African countries.

Significant leaps on the democracy scale have been
made among African countries, even though their development
scores have either remained the same or have actually deteri-
oted (see figure 3.2 for the dynamics of the continental relationship between democracy and development). Mali and Benin
for instance, whose HDI scores have declined, rather shot up
dramatically on the democracy scale. Senegal retained its position while Cape Verde, Congo and Sao Tome experienced a
positive move on both the democracy and HDI scales. Botswana and Mauritius remain the two highest African countries
on both scales. The above illustrations support the view that
while globally, development correlates strongly with democracy, the same cannot be said for Africa. The African pattern is
an intriguing one. While Botwsana and Mauritius have had
sustainable high levels of democracy and development, Senegal
has managed a relatively high level of democracy without any
significant level of development.

On the other hand, Mali and Benin have increased dramatically their levels of democracy with rather declining levels
of development. Zambia, falling on the development scale,
made a major leap on the democracy scale in 1990. Ghana
managed to climb the democracy scale with a slightly significant decline on the development scale. Gambia had managed
to maintain a high level of democracy with a low level of development.[5]

The ambivalent correlation results call for a cautious
interpretation. Higher levels of development may not be needed
for democracy in the short run. But the final failure of democracy in Gambia in 1994 suggests that development in the long
run is necessary for democratic consolidation. In fact, contrary
to the dominant democratic theory, a decline in development
initiates protests for democracy. But the association of higher
levels of development with long sustained democracies in Bot-

Samuel Ebow Quainoo

swana and Mauritius for example, indicate that development is necessary for democratic consolidation.

There are, however, some countries with relatively higher scores of development without a commensurate level of democracy. Gabon for instance scores .51 on the development scale with only a 4.0 score on the democracy scale. Zimbabwe scores .41 on the development scale with only 3.5 on the democracy scale. This phenomena suggests that development is not a sufficient condition for democratic condition. Development combines with other variables for consolidation of democracy on the continent. What other variables then, are needed for democratic consolidation?

## Figure 3.1
## GLOBAL RELATIONSHIPS BETWEEN DEMOCRACY AND HUMAN DEVELOPMENT INDEX, 1990

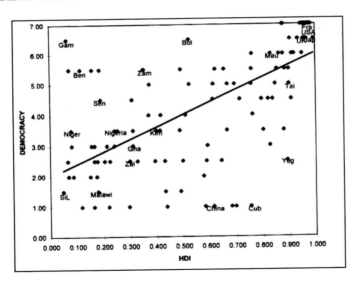

Sources: United Nations Development program and Raymond Gastil.

Countries are identified with the first three letters, except where more than one country shares the first three letters.

## Figure 3.2
## RELATIONSHIP BETWEEN DEMOCRACY
## AND HUMAN DEVELOPMENT INDEX
## IN AFRICA 1990

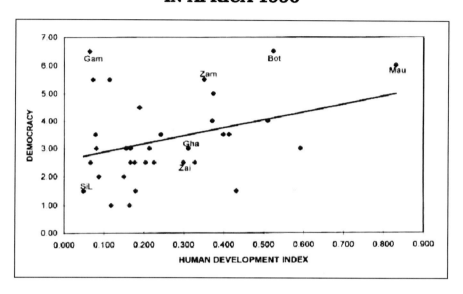

Sources: United Nations Development Program and Raymond Gastil.

Their first three letters represent countries.

*Ethnicity.* One of the most discussed variables connected with democracy in Africa is ethnicity. Many democratically constituted governments have been brought down by ethnically motivated military coups, civil and secession wars. Authoritarian regimes have consistently relied on ethnicity to perpetuate themselves in power. Nigeria suffered a major democratic setback after independence, including the loss of over one million lives when internal conflicts ended in a very costly war (see Herbert Ekwe-Ekwe, 1990). It was essentially an eth-

nic war of secession. Somalia, Angola, Liberia and many others
have followed this disastrous path ever since.

One-party states have been instituted in many plural
societies because of the desire of one or a few ethnic groups to
dominate others. Zimbabwe under Mugabe has often threat-
ened to establish a one-party system. Ethnic tensions and conflicts have increasingly become the bane of democracy in Africa
and other parts of the world. What are the roots of these ethnic
tensions and conflicts?

Colonialism has often become the scape-goat for explanations of ethnic conflicts in post-independent Africa. Arguments abound to the effect that the arbitrary partition of Africa
among the colonial powers separated groups which were together, and put together groups which historically have been at
each others' throats. The "artificiality of boundaries" thesis
cites the discrepancies in ethnic and political frontiers as the
cause of the ethnic conflicts (R. N. Ismagilova, 1978).

It was such a troubling issue for African countries fighting for their independence, that a declaration was issued at the
*All African Peoples Conference* held in the then only independent sub-Saharan country (Ghana) in 1958. According to a report by Theobald in *The New Nations of West Africa* (1960, p.
149),

> The Conference: (a) denounces artificial frontiers
> drawn by imperialist powers to divide the peoples of
> Africa, particularly those which cut across ethnic
> groups and people of the same stock; (b) calls for the
> abolition or adjustment of such frontiers at an early
> date.

Soon thereafter in 1963, when these same leaders became the Heads of State of their respective countries after independence, they met in Addis Ababa and firmly supported the
boundaries that had previously been condemned. The newly
born *Organization of African Unity* (OAU), which was comprised
of all independent African nations, proclaimed the opposite in
one of the basic principles of its charter. Item 3 of Article 3
asks member countries to:

respect the sovereignty and territorial integrity of each State and for its inalienable right to its independent existence.

The possibility of reversing colonial boundaries is dim. Arguing for ethnic unity in the form of one ethnic group in a nation or a nation of only compatible ethnic groups is unreasonable. A re-demarcation exercise would be messy and counter-productive. There would hardly be a single viable nation in Africa. For instance, the Fulani people can be found in modern day Guinea, Cameroon and Nigeria. The Ewes can now be traced to Ghana, Togo and Nigeria. The Hausas occupy Nigeria, Ghana and Niger. Without massive disruptions of lives, there is no possible way of re-drawing national boundaries to re-group compatible ethnic groups.

The question then arises, that if the people and their leaders understand this ethnic phenomena and its ramifications, why the proliferation of ethnic conflicts in post-independent Africa? Perhaps focusing on ethnic fractionalization as the basis of ethnic conflict and threats to democracy is misleading.

Empirical evidence on ethnic conflicts in Africa suggest that it is not necessarily caused by the mere division of ethnic groups into many different countries by colonial boundaries. Gambia, Senegal and Ghana among others who have ethnic groups living in neighboring countries, and are themselves ethnically heterogenous, have managed to avoid serious ethnic conflicts since independence over thirty years ago.

Major threats to democracy have not come from just the ethnic composition of a country. Ethnic carnage has occurred in countries of all type of ethnic compositions. It is interesting to note that the recent ethnic wars in Rwanda and Burundi were not about the creation of separate states for the Tutsis and the Hutsis. It was mainly about gaining equal access to the political process in a country where one group had monopolized political power. This is not to argue that there has not been seccessional demands. There have been some demands but with the exception of Eritrea, the colonial boundaries have held very well, given its high levels of artificiality.

Quite unlike the Bosnia situation outside Africa, Africa's ethnic problems have generally had a different orientation.

Pre-colonial Africa had its ethnic conflicts. In Ghana for instance, the Ashantis' expansionist tendencies had engaged them in several battles with the other groups in the area, especially the coastal Fantis and the Ewes. Unfortunately, the colonial era witnessed, in some cases, a deliberate, and in others, unintended deepening of already existing ethnic rifts, either to maximize profits at minimum administrative cost or to create ethnic buffer zones between themselves (the colonial power) and the potentially 'trouble-making' ethnic groups.

In Ghana, the coastal Fantis had unparalleled access to education, helping them to benefit disproportionately from the recruitment to the newly Africanized civil service positions, to the detriment of the other ethnic groups. In Uganda, the Baganda were appointed as deputies and tax collectors among the Nilots. In Guinea the Fulbe got the nod from the French colonial authorities to work as civil servants among the Gerze, Toma, Konyagi and the Bassari (Ismagilova 1978).

Such colonial policies created uneven socio-economic development among ethnic groups that carried through to the newly independent administrations. During the struggle for independence, nationalist leaders managed to unite the people of all ethnic persuasions to fight off the colonial yoke. The socio-economic differences and the imminent bitterness were ignored by post colonial national governments. It was obvious that the leaders were aware of this problem and the danger it posed to national unity and development. The 1969 commission set by the Togolese government to study the North-South problem concluded, as reported in West Africa, (5th April, 1969, p. 395), that the socio-economic imbalance between the two has fostered;

> social upheavals which often turn into tribal and ethnic conflicts, aggravated by the shortage of jobs and the people's very small purchasing power.

The benign neglect of this serious continental problem and its blatant exploitation of it by some national leaders to perpetuate themselves in power are the root causes of the current destabilizing conflicts in Africa, and not necessarily the ethnic composition of the countries.

Some leaders aware of its consequences, made serious efforts to address the situation. Kwame Nkrumah of Ghana, for instance, coming from a very small minority group himself, introduced a form of an *Affirmative Action program* in the 1960s where everyone from the poorer Northern region was given free scholarships from the primary level up to the University level.[6] This was a laudable strategy to narrow the gap in educational opportunities that existed between the north and the south immediately after independence.

Those leaders who did not address this issue seriously gave the deprived groups and their leaders the cause to perceive themselves as excluded from the benefits of the national cake and therefore paved the way for confrontations along ethnic lines. A majority of the ethnic conflagrations have had similar backgrounds. Ethnic heterogeneity by itself therefore need not be a hindrance to democratic governance unless the leadership and the institutions blatantly exploit the imminent divisions and exclude some groups from gaining access to political power. Ethnic divisions are not the only social problem that have produced political conflict and hurt the chances of democracy.

*Religion.* Religion has caused its fair share of political conflicts. Different religions have been described as either conducive or as a hindrance to democracy because of the dictates of their doctrines. Huntington's (1984) study among others, focus on religion and democracy. He argues that religions that are extremely hierarchical and expect total obedience from a god hinder the development of democracy.

According to his study, Protestantism strongly correlates with democracy, while Islam, Confucianism, and Buddhism are highly conducive to authoritarianism. He further contends that while Catholicism's relation with democracy is ambivalent, Hindu and Shinto cultures are more tolerant to diversity and social change and therefore are amenable to democracy. In Africa, most of the religious conflicts have been between Islam and Christianity.

Islam, in particular, has been cited as a religion which is not receptive to democracy because of its doctrinal rigidity (see for example, Daniel Pipes, 1989). There is supposed to be a restriction on political participation with the power of decision-making deferred to God, since Islam means a total surrender to Allah. Human power is viewed with suspicion since it is believed to be tainted with selfish individual or class interests. Islam is therefore seen as not compatible with democratic rule. Do these findings hold in Africa? Has Islam been a hindrance to democracy in Africa? Does Christianity in Africa have a better record with regard to democracy?

An examination of the relationship between Islam, Christianity, and African traditional religions reveals an ambivalent result. Relying on the Gastil's democracy data set and World Factbook and Encyclopedia of the Third World, it is observed that no one particular religion has a monopoly on democracy (see table 3.3 for religious composition of states and figure 3.3 for their positions on the democracy scale).[7] Does this invalidate the findings of earlier studies that posit strong relationships between religion and democracy? Do foreign religions have a different impact on Africa? It may be argued that the influence of foreign religions' on Africa may be superficial. African traditional religions are polytheistic in nature and easily incorporate other foreign religions such as Islam and Christianity. Even though the two Abrahamic religions are monotheistic, most African Christians and Muslims convert to them and still retain some aspects of their traditional religions. In this regard, Christianity and Islam have become Africanized, diluting the rigidity of the original doctrines. The tolerant nature of African traditional religions may therefore be responsible for the African deviation from the global norm.

## Figure 3.3
## IDENTIFICATION OF RELIGION ON
## DEMOCRACY/LITERACY GRAPH, 1990

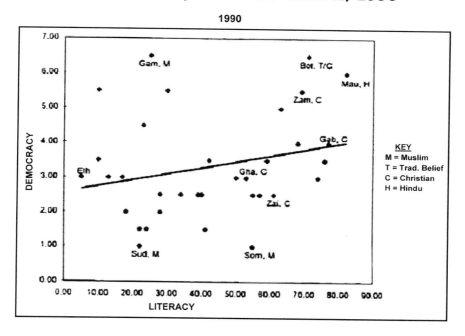

Sources: UNESCO, R. Gastil and World Fact Handbook.

Countries are identified by their first three letters.

*Colonial Heritage.* Does a country's colonial background influence its future prospect for democratic governance? Do former British colonies have a better chance at democracy than former French colonies? It has been argued that the British colonial policies did not tamper with established institutions of authority and therefore post-colonial British Africa, with many of their traditions intact, had an easier chance of building upon those institutions which were democratic in nature (See for example, Myron Weiner, 1988). Of particular interest is the

'Indirect Rule' policy introduced by Lord Lugard in Northern Nigeria, where the Emirs were left in charge of the day-to-day governing of their peoples.[8] The traditional political system was therefore not disrupted, avoiding some of the foundational problems new systems encounter.

The French, on the other hand, wanted an assimilation of their colonial subjects into French culture. The belief in the superiority of French culture encouraged a wholesale tampering of traditions including indigenous political structures. When General Charles De Gaulle finally gave in to the demands for independence in Francophone Africa, the dependence on the French political structures was imminent, making the task of building democratic structures from the start more daunting.

## Table 3.3
### Religion and Democracy in 1990

| COUNTRY | DEMOCRACY SCORE | RELIGION |
|---|---|---|
| Botswana | 6.50 | Indigenous/ Christian |
| Mauritius | 6.00 | Hindu |
| Gambia | 6.50 | Islam |
| Benin | 5.50 | Indigenous |
| Mali | 5.50 | Islam |
| Zambia | 5.50 | Indigenous |
| Senegal | 4.00 | Islam |
| Guinea | 2.50 | Islam |
| Uganda | 2.50 | Christian |
| Togo | 2.50 | Islam |
| Malawi | 1.50 | Christian |
| Sierra Leone | 1.50 | Indigenous |
| Liberia | 1.50 | Indigenous |

Sources: Raymond Gastil's Freedom of the World Data 1990, *World Factbook* (1987) and *Encyclopedia of the Third World* (1987) Arthur Bank's *Political Handbook of the World* (1995)

Key: Religion of a country is determined by the percentage of the dominant religion.

Utilizing Gastil's democracy scores once again, it becomes evident that there is no discernible pattern regarding the relationship of colonial heritage and democracy. While former British colonies fair slightly better in democratic sustenance, they do not establish a clear monopoly (table 3.4 illustrates this point by providing democracy scores of some of the countries with the highest and lowest scores and their former colonial ties). While it is fair to argue that Botswana's relationship with Britain, for instance, helped it to retain its traditional democratic system, it is more of the quality of the elite leadership in post-independent Botswana that should be credited with its political achievement. Senegal accepted the cultural baggage of France during the colonial rule, but its democracy record is more appreciable than many former British colonies. Mauritius, which came under the influence of both Britain and France, utilizes aspects of both heritages, but their democratic record is also more attributable to elite leadership than to cultural heritage.

## Table 3.4
### *Democracy and Colonial Heritage*

| COUNTRY | DEMOCRACY SCORE | FORMER COLONIAL POWER |
|---|---|---|
| Botswana | 6.50 | British |
| Mauritius | 6.00 | British/French |
| Gambia | 6.50 | British |
| Benin | 5.50 | French |
| Mali | 5.50 | French |
| Zambia | 5.50 | British |
| Senegal | 4.00 | French |
| Guinea | 2.50 | French |
| Uganda | 2.50 | British |
| Togo | 2.50 | French |
| Malawi | 1.50 | British |
| Sierra Leone | 1.50 | British |
| Liberia | 1.50 | * |

Sources: Raymond Gastil's *Freedom of the World Scores*, 1990; Arthur Bank's *Political Handbook of the World*, 1995.

* Liberia was never a colony.

## Conclusion

In sum, ethnic heterogeneity and the dispersal of ethnic groups into different countries by themselves do not create the conflicts which have been a hindrance to the development of democracy in Africa. The threat of ethnicity to democracy will not come from the mere composition of a country's ethnic grouping but from the policies and effectiveness of the institutions that are established to regulate the inevitable competition.

The artificiality of the borders, as disturbing as it is, may not be the major culprit for democratic failure. Disadvantaged ethnic groups feel excluded from the affairs of the state when the socio-economic structures limit their access and deprive them of their fair share of the national cake. In most cases, when constitutions, institutions and policies have been crafted to incorporate effectively all groups as in Mauritius for example, a political glue has been found to keep groups together for peaceful co-existence. Democracy, contrary to its competitive nature, offers a better opportunity in regulating these social tensions than authoritarianism, which relies on suppression.

Being a former British or French colony may only help in building democracy if the leadership (individuals and groups) develop a strong commitment to policies of inclusion. Economic development on the other hand will be needed in the long run if democracy is to be consolidated. But all these factors will be shaped by the type of democratic transition a country undergoes. This will be the focus of the next chapter.

## Notes to Chapter Three

1.  The HDI is based on three indicators: longevity (life expectancy at birth), educational attainment (adult literacy and combined primary, secondary and tertiary enrollment ratios), and standard of living (GDP per capita). The Index is constructed by fixing minimum and maximum values for these

indicators. For any component of the HDI, individual indices are computed with a general formula:

$$\frac{Actual\ x1\ value - minimum\ x1\ value}{Maximum\ x1\ value - minumum\ x1\ value}$$

The HDI is a simple average of the indices of the three components lready mentioned. It is calculated by dividing the sum of the three indices by 3. The higher the number, the higher the level of development. For a detailed explanation of HDI computation, see *Human Development Report, 1992*.

2.  Other measures being used as indicators for development include the Physical Quality of Life Index (PQLI). The index is based on three indicators: infant mortality, life expectancy and literacy. It measures socio-economic activities of a country. See for example, Hofferbert and Cingranelli, an unpublished paper for WPSA in 1988.

3.  The global correlation of HDI and democracy is strong and fairly consistent. For 1970, 1980 and 1990, the correlation has been 0.54, 0.63 and 0.64 respectively. It hides the dynamics of regional situations.

4.  The partition of Africa took place in the nineteenth century in Europe among European colonial powers. The partition was done without any regard to ethnic or cultural compatibility.

5.  Gambia's long standing democracy came to a halt in 1994 with a military coup toppling the elected president and the cabinet. The constitution has been suspended indefinetely.

6.  Education from the primary to the tertiary level is free in Ghana. Those from the 'North' enjoy further breaks, such as transportation and clothing allowances, because of the higher poverty levels of the region.

7.  Islam and Christianity are the only two major foreign religions in Africa. There are more Christian countries in Africa, but in population, the figure may be closer because of the

size of Muslims in Nigeria, the most densely populated country in Africa.

8.  The British 'respect' for traditional authority structures did not have any cultural motivations. It was purely out of prudence and the desire to save administrative cost.

## Questions to Chapter Three

1. What are the variables that affect democracy?

2. Explain why the HDI is a better measure of development than the GDP or GNI.

## CHAPTER FOUR
# TRANSITIONS

## Introduction

The spontaneity and simultaneity of the current transitions to democracy in Africa give the erroneous impression that they all follow one path and have the same dynamics. They may all have been influenced by socio-economic conditions and external factors, but the actual transition processes are influenced by many country-specific factors. Transitions have different dynamics. Transition style also affects the pace, path, and outcome of the democratization process in general. It is therefore imperative to examine individual transitions critically to understand better the democratization efforts unfolding in Africa.

Attempts have been made, mostly by scholars of Southern European and Latin American politics, to study transition styles and outcomes (see for example, Guillermo O'Donnell and Philippe C. Schmitter, 1986). Since the 1960 transitions from colonial rule to independent nations, no major democratic transitions have taken place on the continent, hence the lack of research focus on African transitions.[1]

Many theories have been advanced to differentiate between types of transitions (see for instance, Geoffrey Pridham, 1991). While some have been distinguished according to their pace, others have been characterized by their leadership styles. Even though each transition has its own uniqueness, there are many commonalities among them. In Africa, there have been two broad patterns, one planned and controlled by elite groups and the other forced by events without prior planned strategy and leadership. This study will group African patterns under two main types, *top-down* and *bottom-up* transitions.

## Transition Types

The adoption of these divisions is informed by the *Contingent Choice theory*. This theory places the outcomes of transitions on the decisions made by both the authoritarian regime and the pro-democracy advocates. It argues that the outcome of a transition depends on the negotiations conducted among the major participants of the exercise.[2]

Political change in Africa has been highly influenced by individual leaders and elite groups. This phenomena may have its roots in the traditional authority structures where more often than not, the survival or flourishing of a group depended on the chief or king. Colonialism was ended in many cases by individual acts of heroism or commitment, giving birth to the concept of *founding-fathers* in post-colonial Africa.[3] In post-colonial Africa, individuals or elite leaderships influence the type of political changes that take place on the continent. The current transitions to democracy will not be understood without an examination of the role played by key political actors, hence the adoption of the Contingent Choice theory (which focuses on political actors) for analysis of the process.

*Top-Down Transitions.* Top-down transitions involve degrees of consensus among the elites of the pro-democracy movement and the authoritarian regime. The role of political actors is crucial. First and foremost, the elites must have effective control over their mass supporters or sympathizers. Such control allows them the room for political pact making, and also makes it easier to enforce decisions made on the rest of the people. The South African and Ghanaian transitions are classic examples of countries that adopted the top-down approach to democracy. Their success can partially be attributed to elite consensus, and the presence of relatively organized institutions. Top-down transitions occur mostly under *corporatist* authoritarian regimes. Corporatist regimes are those that have institutions of recognized social representation and control (Baohui Zhang, 1994). Under such regimes, not only do elites have the freedom to negotiate on behalf of the people, their decisions are more easy to enforce. In Ghana for instance, the presence and effectiveness of a well organized Professional Bodies Association (PBA), a politically conscious National Union of Ghanaian Students (NUGS), a strong National House of Chiefs, and an independent judiciary made organized pressure possible on the authoritarian regime. More importantly, it made it easier for smooth elite negotiations, and more effective implementation of transition decisions once an agreement was reached. The recognition and relative trust in organizations and their leadership prevented unnecessary chaos and unchannelled mass disruptions.

The South African transition seemed a lost cause because of the extreme hostility and tension generated by apartheid among the races, and the determination of both camps to have the impending change go their way. The transition was a success because groups were relatively well organized and their leaders had effective control. It can be argued that the control of Chief Buthelezi over the Zulus' Nkatha movement, the credibility of de Klerk among the majority of whites, and the overwhelming sway Mandela had over the African National Congress (which forms the bulk of the population), made it possible to have a relatively smooth transition.

The Ghanaian transition did not experience the level of violence exhibited in South Africa, but it had its share of rancor and bitterness. Politics have always revolved around certain groups, the Nkrumah and Danquah/Busia traditions. Once the elites in these camps accepted the need for a transition, the only point of disagreement was the modalities of the process itself to ensure fairness. An underlying element of top-down transitions is therefore elite consensus.

The authoritarian regime must be made to accept the inevitability of the change towards democracy. The pro-democracy elites, on the other hand, must be prepared to demonstrate some degrees of flexibility, allowing the authoritarian incumbents to retain a number of face-saving privileges. The recent Cedras/Aristide arrangements in Haiti comes readily to mind. Cedras and his close associates had to be allowed a safe passage out of Haiti with U.S. backed assurances of protection for their property. If such privileges had been left for the people to decide, it might have been rejected, threatening the transition in the process. In spite of the desire of the majority of the ANC to nationalize and re-distribute land which had been taken away by an unjust apartheid system, and in spite of the strong intransigence of some of the white South Africans to preserve the privileges of the status quo, the elites of both races realized the impossibility of sticking to such extreme positions, and consented to giving up some of the aspirations of their supporters for the success of a transition.

Top-down transitions, by their very nature, restrict participation during the period of negotiations. The level of democracy immediately after the transition may not be high. Concessions may have to be made to the authoritarian regime, to solicit its cooperation in the transition. The legitimacy of the authoritarian regime is not totally destroyed, remnants of undemocratic practices may remain. Such concessions are however necessary in the short run to buy off the authoritarian elites; hence de Klerk, who headed the government of Apartheid South Africa, still retained a top position in the newly democratic government, and Rawlings, who had led the previous authoritarian military regime in Ghana, was allowed to contest for the presidency in the newly established democratic system.

As stated initially, less democratic gains are achieved under the top-down transitions but it is at the cost of ensuring a smoother path towards consolidation. The democratic gains under top-down transitions are rather incremental unlike the bottom up approach which ideally makes a clean break with its all-or-nothing demand. With time however, top-down transitions accumulate more democratic gains as the new systems acquire roots, phasing out the remaining vestiges of authoritarianism.

*Bottom-up Transitions.* Bottom-up transitions occur when authoritarian regimes lose control and are swept out of office by a spontaneous event or a series of them, not expected by the incumbent. Normally, such occurrences are not planned. Not much negotiations take place, with the transition process following the dictates of the people, without the involvement of recognized leaders at the initial stage.

Usually, bottom-up transitions occur in societies that have been subjected to long periods of authoritarian rule. Proto-democratic organizations and institutions are absent, creating structural problems for the leaders who finally emerge from the process. The regime's control of the society is pervasive and through forms of intimidation and sometimes ruthless force, any associational activity that is found to be threatening to the regime is suppressed.

In place of civic organizations, *auxiliary institutions* are set up by the regime for inculcating "national consciousness and pride," which inevitably become instruments of intimidation. *The Young Pioneers Movement* and the *Peoples Defence Committees* under Ghana's Kwame Nkrumah and Jerry Rawlings respectively, are classical examples of such auxilliary institutions. Membership of these organizations come with a lot of privileges, in return for loyalty to the repressive regime. The net effect is the loss of civic space which is needed for expressions against state abuses. Zaire, and Zambia under Kenneth Kaunda (to some extent) exemplify such societies.

In such societies, authoritarian leaders have firm control to the extent that when protests for democracy break out finally, they are surprised and caught unprepared to negotiate for a planned exit. When mass movements succeed in extracting reforms from the regime, the emerging leaders neither have the needed institutional channels to direct their demands nor the organizational coherence to consolidate and build on their gains. No clear-cut leaders with the prior support and recognition from the people is apparent and the transitional exercise gets captured by the mood swings of the people.

Although Kaunda's rule in Zambia limited the civic space needed for the challenge of authoritarian rule, two institutions refused to be denied their space. The trade unions, especially those of the miners, organized themselves well. The mining union in particular, played a key role in the transition because of the importance of mining to the Zambian economy. The churches were not direct targets for repression because they were not seen as political threats to Kaunda's authoritarian rule or probably because of Kaunda's personal association

with Christianity. These two organizations became very instrumental in the struggle for democracy. It is not a coincidence that Frederick Chiluba, a Trade Unionist and an ardent
Christian, became the presidential candidate for the democracy advocates.

Societies with thoroughly repressive regimes are left
with no other choice than to adopt a bottom-up approach
when the time comes for a democratic transition. The only alternative left for the organizationally and institutionally unprepared leaders of the societies under such a transition style is to
rely on the "mobilization of collective moral energy, commitment, and dedication" (Jan Pakulski 1988, p. 250). The usefulness of relying solely on the people without identifiable group
leaders and viable institutions is, however, limited. If an institutional framework is not developed in a relatively short time,
the exercise may even be delayed unnecessarily or even be de-
railed.

Bottom-up transitions are more broad-based in terms of
participation. On the surface, this may seem positive because
it is in line with the very tenet of democracy. But the very
broad nature of mass democracy movements and the diversity
of interests they attract can spell doom for new democracies.
The common bond of the mass movements is the hatred of the
incumbent authoritarian regime and its removal becomes the
main goal. Once this objective is achieved, it becomes difficult
to maintain momentum, build loyalty to the new system and
tone down the radical character of the pre-transition activities.

Unlike the top-down transitions which do not rely exclusively on the people in the initial stages, bottom-up transitions are people-driven. More often than not, they do not have
the space and time to settle down, plan and implement their
policies. Leaders are usually creations of the mass movements
and therefore derive their political base from the people. Momentum swings and unrealistic expectations from the people
are therefore a constant worry for the leaders. Elites in the top-
down transitions do not share such vulnerability because of
their effective control over the peoples through the well-estab-
lished institutions and organizations.

It is apparent from the above analysis that the top-down approach has a better chance at a smooth and stable transition to democracy than the bottom-up type. But the decision to adopt a particular transition strategy does not necessarily lie solely with the political actors. The type of authoritarian regime and its long effect on the society play a critical role. A more repressive authoritarian regime does not offer much of a chance in terms of adopting a top-down style towards democracy.

It must be noted, however, that an exceptional leadership can sometimes overcome the structural obstacles that bottom-up transitions present. Complacency and lack of commitment to democracy among elites in top-down transitions can also create problems in the new democracies. In both transition types leadership is crucial. It affects the pace, sequence and outcome of the democratization exercise. A transition can move smoothly, be stifled at a certain stage, or revert to authoritarianism. A discussion of transition phases at this juncture may throw more light on the sequence of events.

## Transition Phases

Defining the chronological boundaries of transition is not an easy task. Pinpointing the time of initiation is problematic, because it rarely involves a single defining event. While usually transitions are initiated by pressures from pro-democracy advocates, there are rare occasions when the authoritarian regime cracks from within, well before the galvanized protests or demands from the outside get to them.

It may be a disagreement among the authoritarian elites themselves, due to a change of perception by some of them, or an admission of failure because of the overwhelming nature of problems. A change of plans among authoritarian elites may also come from an indirect pressure applied from external sources for various reasons.

Determining the end point of a transition, in the same vein, is an arduous task. Does a transition end with the conduct of elections? A delineation of the transition process is, however, necessary for analytical purposes. In reality, the transition process may not neatly follow processes to be described below, or may not even go through all the processes. The earlier stages of the process may be the same for both the top-down and bottom-up transitions.

*Decomposition Stage.* This is the phase when the authoritarian regime begins to doubt itself because of increasingly crippling evidence of failure. Socio-economic conditions start getting worse (not necessarily at its worst point) and pressure from different sources begin to galvanize against the regime.[4] The source of the pressure may be internal (that is within the country), external, or from within the regime itself.

The regime begins to experience legitimacy crises more seriously than before. More repressive strategies may be introduced at this juncture, depending on the type of authoritarian regime to break, intimidate and stifle the opposition.

*Protests Stage.* This is the period when repressive antics of authoritarian regimes fail to weather the political storm, starting a series of public protests. The response will depend on the type of authoritarian regime in place. An inflexible and more repressive regime, failing to recognize the turn in political tides, may introduce further repressive measures. An authoritarian regime which had allowed the development of civic organizations may start courting opposing elites for discussions to resolve problems. Elites rely on intensified protests from all sectors of society including student bodies, religious groups, labor and traditional rulers to press for transition negotiations.

*Liberalization Stage.* A major decision to negotiate is made at this phase by the more flexible authoritarian regime. Small concessions are granted. The more repressive regime does not get to this point. It keeps holding on, believing the protests can be silenced with more repression. In the less repressive environment, foundations of a top-down transition begins to be built. A promise of transition is made and elites of both camps start working out its modalities. An assembly of constitutional experts or a body of the kind is charged with this task. The authoritarian regime makes public gestures to demonstrate good intent. Some of the decisions taken at this stage include lifting the ban on politics if there was one, and softening of stance through public speeches on issues the regime had hitherto been adamant about. For instance, if the notion of multi-party politics had been discredited before, it begins to be portrayed in a more favorable light. In effect, the authoritarian regime begins to position itself for the inevitable elections.

Efforts are made by both camps to cultivate a feeling of goodwill among the people. However, while the authoritarian regime publicly speaks of cooperation, much effort is being made covertly to gain as much advantage as possible through fair and unfair means. The authoritarian regime is at an advantage at this stage as national resources are usually put at the disposal of their openly backed or secretly favored parties. Intimidation continues, albeit a softer and more discreet approach than the hey days of the regime.

*Election Stage.* Bottom-up transitions come to this stage usually direct from the protest stage. Authoritarian regimes become intransigent and refuse to negotiate for a well-planned transition until they are overtaken by events. It may take one decisive event or a series of events to bring the regime down. When it becomes inevitable that elections should be held for a democratic system, both the authoritarian regime and the people who fought for the change are caught unprepared. The change is usually dictated by momentum of the people without any prior recognized leadership. The leader or leaders who emerge among the people are as surprised by the turn of events as is the authoritarian regime who had erroneously believed in its own invincibility.

The top-down transitions, on the other hand, go through the election with the authoritarian regime's favored party competing against the other parties of the pro-democracy advocates. It is not necessarily a clean election as genuine and ill-intentioned mistakes are made because the exercise is relatively new to the population. Election results may be disputed but once a transfer of power is executed peacefully, and a new government is put in place, the transition can be defined as complete (Figures 4.1 and 4.2 provide a clearer picture of the transition path. The main and most crucial difference is the missing Liberalization Stage in bottom-up transitions. This stage is crucial because it determines whether the transition will be relatively well-planned or chaotic).

   *Consolidation.* Consolidation, for the purpose of this analysis is defined simplistically as the successful conduct of three more elections since the transition, following the dictates of the constitution. It indicates the acceptance of the system of changing the government. A third election, with the rules and regulations followed and the result accepted by the majority of the people, legitimizes the system.

## Figure 4.1
## PHASES OF A TOP-DOWN TRANSITION

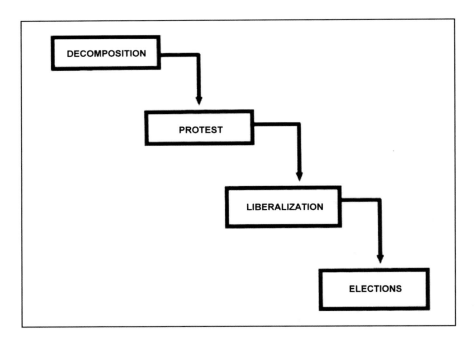

## Figure 4.2
## PHASES OF A BOTTOM-UP TRANSITION

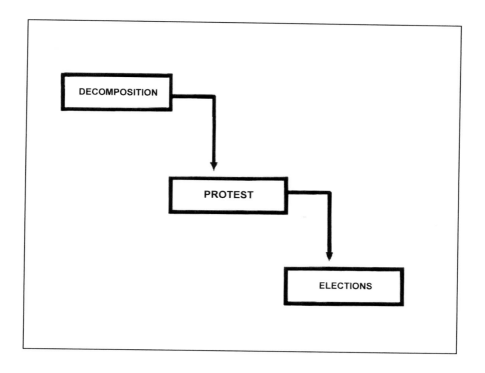

Should there be a turn-over in government before a democracy is certified as consolidated? If the elections are certified to be free and fair, with the opposition having a chance for success, then there is no need for the turn-over criteria. The electorate may choose to return the incumbent as many times as the constitution allows. Sweden has been under the Social Democrats for many years, and it is still considered a consolidated democracy.

Defining consolidation the way the study does is useful for the purpose of establishing chronological parameters of the democratization process for analytical purposes. However, for a democracy to be accepted as the permanent system of government of a country, it involves the presence of certain structural conditions and a civil society. Structural conditions such as proto-democratic institutions will be discussed in a later chapter. The presence of structural conditions will, however, achieve little for both top-down and bottom-up transitions if the society has no reasonable level of civility. What then constitutes a civil society and what is its contribution to democratic sustenance?

*Civil Society and Democracy.* Civil society is not a sufficient condition for the consolidation of democracy. It acts as a catalyst to democratic consolidation. The role of civil society in democratic polities has received much attention in the social sciences lately (see for example, Diamond, 1994).[5] Diamond argues, in the same vein as many others, that civil society serves as a major means of exposing the abuses and the undemocratic practices of an authoritarian regime. Civil society helps sustain democracy by monitoring and restraining the exercise of power by states. Diamond (p. 5) characterizes civil society as:

> the realm of organized social life that is voluntary,
> self-generating, autonomous from the state, and
> bound by a legal order or set of shared rules.

Civil society is that part of society which has its own life distinctly and largely autonomous from the state. It provides the fillip for the effective functioning of autonomous economic and social institutions. Its relationship with the state is complex.

While it is distinct from the state, civil society is not entirely separate from the state. It operates within the legal boundaries set by the state; on the other hand, civil society also sets limits on the powers of the state. The state and civil society are related by the constraints put on them by the constitution. They both seek to protect and strengthen the rights of citizens as individuals and as collectivities.

A society which is civil observes decorum in managing competition and resolving its conflicts without often resorting to violence. There are bound to be serious disagreements in the allocation of limited resources in any society which has diverse interest groups with differing perceptions. Given the empirical fact that there is hardly a society homogenous enough not to have such differences, especially so in modern urban societies, there ought to be some means of resolving the unavoidable conflicts of interests without destruction of life and property.

When the resolution of ensuing conflicts are conducted by members of the society generally with the awareness, understanding and regard to the rule of law, a civil society is said to be in place. Rule of law is not solely enforced by instruments of force but by the conscience of the society as well. Such conduct of behavior occurs among individuals, between groups and finally between these individuals and groups towards the state and vice versa.

In civil societies, the autonomy of the state is respected. Civil society operates within the legal framework set by the state. In the same vein, the law binds the state in its treatment of the citizens. It protects the individual from arbitrary and unjust treatment from the state or agents of the state. A respected state which recognizes the boundaries of its institutions, and a civil citizenry which is well-informed of its duties and responsibilities towards the state and its agencies, provide a strong foundation for a permanent acceptance of democracy.

A respect for the rule of law and the legitimacy of the state is very crucial in creating a civil society. Edward Shils (1991, p. 16) captures this point when he asserts that,

> the tendency towards law abidingness must be reinforced by belief in the legitimacy of the laws or the regulations. Legitimacy in a pluralistic, civil society depends on the civil attachments of the bulk of the citizenry to the central institutions of society.

The state and the laws it enacts will be perceived as legitimate only when the citizenry believes that the government and the political institutions seek their interest. The African state has its peculiar problems. Peter Lewis (1992, p. 40) for instance, in a cross regional analysis of state-society relations of Africa, East Asia, and Latin America, characterizes the African polity as "distinguished by limited degrees of state hegemony, a narrow range of political inclusion and highly tenuous engagement with autonomous societal groups."

Colonialism has the original blame for the state problem in Africa. The problem of European colonizers carving societies with total disregard for ethnic, religious and linguistic harmony has been discussed in the earlier chapters. The initial low levels of attachment to the modern African state by the people is understandable. But three decades after independence should have seen a more significant change in the relationship between the state and the society. While it may be true that the colonial era saw a deliberate attempt by the colonizers at suppressing citizen participation and involvement in the affairs of the state, hampering the creation of a viable civic space in the process, post-colonial Africa has not done enough to reverse this negative state-society relationship.

The modern African state has been weakened further by the divisive policies of the post-independent governments. The weak and fragmented state inherited from the colonizers became exacerbated when rigid patrimonial systems were immediately put into place in the newly independent states. Access to state revenues and other national resources came to be controlled by the personalized ruler and his cronies. Such patterns created a society-state dependency syndrome where two unhealthy options developed. Economic survival depended on one's unflinching and often blinding loyalty to the state which became synonymous with the ruler. This route remains the main option for individual or group interests to be addressed. The second option is to refuse such sycophantic approaches to economic survival and in the process disengage oneself or the group from the state.

Both options are detrimental to the creation of a civil society. The first option leaves little room for the development of a viable economic private sector, with enough resources to challenge the pervasive role of the state. Most economic activities become controlled by the state, encouraging cronyism, nepotism and corruption. The result is a reduction of the civic space and the resource base needed to challenge the arbitrariness of state power. The second option of disengagement from the state reduces the legitimacy of the state and the laws it enacts. The rule of law suffers, as the majority of citizens who are not political clients of the state with its personalized authority do not perceive the laws to be in their interest. The state faces legitimacy problems and its relationship with society becomes anything but civil. What are the specific contributions of civil society to democratic consolidation?

Diamond argues that a vibrant civil society is essential for consolidating democracy rather than initiating it. Most of the new democracies in Africa have just put into place political and economic institutions to regulate society under a democratic system. Given the pervasiveness of patrimonial relationships in the previous regimes and the lack of appreciable levels of economic development, containing political corruption initially may be a serious problem. A civil society may play a vital role not only in containing the power of the newly democratic governments, but also in helping to strengthen the legal and bureaucratic institutions that protect the interest of the citizenry.

A civil society also breeds many associations which cut across class, ethnic, religious and regional lines. Members of such associations come from diverse backgrounds and it takes a cultivation of virtues of tolerance and moderation to bring them together and maintain them. Democratic procedures are mostly employed in running these associations. A significant number of such associations can inculcate the ideals and practice of democracy in the society through its members.

An introduction of such ideals in the political system may therefore not seem too alien to the members of these associations. Many such associations abound in the new African democracies, especially in Ghana, and Zambia to some extent. In Zambia, women's organizations and churches played pivotal roles in the recent transition to democracy. In Ghana, such associations do not only operate in the country but also in foreign lands. Ghanaian foreign associations usually take on the duty of financing development projects at home. Their material contribution allows them to have a significant say in the running of the government back home. Such roles played by civic organizations give them a leverage to constrain the government on occasions of power abuse.

The revolution in information technology has increased transparency of governments and it is also helping in the inculcation of civility among citizens. For example, the Ghanaian electronic network *Okyeame*, which links Ghanaian students and professionals all over the world, provides a forum for robust debates and discussions about Ghana. Grouping Ghanaians of all ethnic, religious, and professional backgrounds, it advocates tolerance, openness, and respect for all views on all issues. The appointment of an eminent electronic postmaster on the network has ensured a civil engagement of diverse ideas and this has become a forum for acquiring political skills needed in a democracy. There are other similar networks for many other African countries. This brings to the fore an important ingredient in a civil society, namely the dissemination of information.

Effective dissemination of information in a society of diverse interests and composition is essential to avoid misunderstanding and suspicion. It promotes accountability and transparency, qualities that are the foundation of democracy. But does the mere availability of information help democracy? While a vibrant free press is crucial in the dissemination of information, one needs to be functionally literate to avail oneself of the benefits of information provided.

## Literacy Rates and Civil Society

A well-informed society has a higher chance of learning more about themselves and from others, in the process appreciating a diversity of viewpoints and enjoying higher levels of tolerance. Information about the government activities and the society in general also helps in the understanding of how the government works. It further educates the citizenry about their rights and responsibilities, and encourages them to challenge the government when their rights are trampled upon. A common national means of communication is vital for such an exercise. In this regard, the extremely high levels of Africa's linguistic heterogeneity has been a problem.

Africa is the cradle of languages. Morrison et al. (1989) confirm that Africa has the highest number of languages per capita of any area in the world. With most Africans being multi-lingual, the absence of one national language of communication understood by all, is a hindrance to the creation of a national democratic political culture. Even though foreign languages (notably English, French, and Portuguese) have been adopted as national languages with the exception of a few countries, they are not spoken and understood by all the population. This has been an obstacle in forging a stronger link among different ethno-linguistic groups.

Relying on the literacy rates in 1990 provided by United Nations Educational Scientific and Cultural Organization (UNESCO) and the democracy data, it is observed that most countries that score high on the democracy scale, also have relatively high literacy rates (see table 4.1).

Of particular interest is the strength of relationship between literacy rates and democracies that are consolidated. Stable democracies such as Botswana and Mauritius for instance, have relatively high literacy rates of 71% and 82% respectively. It can be argued therefore, that a higher literacy rate increases the level of civility in a society by making information more accessible to a larger population. The level of civility and the literacy rates of societies are therefore important keys to democratic consolidation.

## Conclusion

Contingency choice theory offers a theoretical base to explain the current transitions in Africa because of its emphasis on the role played by political actors. Politics in Africa in one form or the other, has essentially been dominated by individual rulers or elites, hence the usefulness of the theory which focuses on political actors in political development.

Transitions may be classified as top-down or bottom-up, depending on the presence or absence of recognized elite groups, level of repression of the authoritarian regime, and the existence of certain political structures in the society. In corporate societies where there are recognized elite groups, transitions are negotiated smoothly with authoritarian regimes. In the non-corporate societies, transitions are dominated by the people, with some ill-prepared people finally thrusted into leadership roles. The success rate of such transitions is low because of its lack of planning and commitment from recognized leaders of the society. Transition type also considerably affects the chronology of events.

## Table 4.1
### Democracy and Literacy Rates (1990)

| COUNTRY | LIT. | DEM. |
| --- | --- | --- |
| Angola | 28 | 2.0 |
| Benin | 30 | 5.5 |
| Botswana* | 71 | 6.5 |
| Burkina Faso | 13 | 3.0 |
| Burundi | 34 | 2.5 |
| Cameroon | 55 | 2.5 |
| Chad | 18 | 2.0 |
| Congo | 63 | 5.0 |
| Ethiopia | 50 | 3.0 |
| Gabon | 77 | 4.0 |
| Gambia | 25 | 6.5 |
| Ghana | 53 | 3.0 |
| Guinea | 28 | 2.5 |
| Kenya | 59 | 3.5 |
| Lesotho | 74 | 3.0 |
| Liberia | 22 | 1.5 |
| Madagascar | 68 | 4.0 |
| Malawi | 41 | 1.5 |

## Table 4.1 (continued)
### *Democracy and Literacy Rates (1990)*

| COUNTRY | LIT. | DEM. |
|---|---|---|
| Mali | 10 | 5.5 |
| Mauritius* | 82 | 6.0 |
| Mozambique | 17 | 3.0 |
| Niger | 10 | 3.0 |
| Nigeria | 42 | 3.5 |
| Rwanda | 50 | 3.0 |
| Senegal | 23 | 4.5 |
| Sierra Leone | 24 | 1.5 |
| Somalia | 55 | 1.0 |
| Togo | 39 | 2.5 |
| Uganda | 57 | 2.5 |
| Zaire | 61 | 2.5 |
| Zambia | 69 | 5.5 |
| Zimbabwe | 76 | 3.5 |

Source: UNESCO
*Consolidated Democracies

The consolidation of a democracy will depend on many factors (to be discussed in a later chapter), but civil society is a *sine qua non* for a permanent acceptance of a democratic system. Among other functions it educates the citizenry about the practice of democracy through its civic organizations. It also challenges attempts at abuses by the state and its agencies. Civic societies flourish under societies with high literacy rates.

## Case Studies

Theories are important for analysis in cross national studies. Theorizing involves generalization which gives the freedom to establish areas of commonalities among countries and also highlight points of departures. But there is also the need to test the derived theories on specific countries. Not only will understanding be enhanced that way, but important details that get lost in cross national studies can be brought forward and examined critically.

The first two cases are selected to illustrate the assertions made earlier about the relationship between socio-economic decline and democratic transitions. It has also been argued that Africa's transitions exhibit two main styles, top-down and bottom-up. The study selects Ghana and Zambia to illustrate these transitional styles.

Ghana, one of the countries that has undergone a transition is a classic type of a top-down transition because of the dominance of the elites in the transition process. Grassroot participation was limited, leaving the elites much room for negotiations. The relatively small gain of 0.5 in democracy (see Table 4.2) is indicative of the control still held by the authoritarian regime immediately after a transition. Ghana completely changed its political system without serious changes in political and civil rights, a classic characteristic of top-down transitions.

Zambia is the exact opposite of Ghana. Having been subjected to an authoritarian rule for more than three decades, Zambia executed a transition with a relatively big democratic gain of 2.5, well above the 0.84 African average (see table 4.2). Such a big gain in a short time is a classic feature of bottom-up transitions. The transitions are grassroot dominated as political rights and civil liberties are extended to majority of the people right from the initial stages.

Mali and Benin enjoyed higher democratic gains than Zambia but Zambia's transition is a better case for illustration because of its degree of difficulty. It has been under a dominant leader since its birth as a nation about thirty years ago. It has also experienced economic turn-overs, from one of Africa's best economies to one of its worst. At the time of transition, Zambia was experiencing one of its worst socio-economic down-turns as a nation, making it a prime candidate for the illustration of our theory on socio-economic frustrations. Ghana and Zambia offer the two best cases for examining the transitional styles and the conditions that influenced them.

### Table 4.2
### *Cases for Transition Study*

| COUNTRY | DEMOCRACY 1980 1990 | SCORE DIFFERENCE |
|---------|---------------------|------------------|
| Ghana | 2.5  3.0 | 0.5 |
| Zambia | 2.5  5.5 | 2.5 |

Source: Raymond Gastil (1980, 1990).

### Table 4.3
### *Cases for Consolidation Study*

| COUNTRY | DEMOCRACY 1980 1990 | SCORE AVERAGE |
|---------|---------------------|---------------|
| Bostwana | 5.5  6.5 | 6.0 |
| Mauritius | 6.0  6.0 | 6.0 |

Source: Raymond Gastil (1980, 1990).

The second two cases are meant to probe for conditions that facilitate consolidated democracy. Under what conditions have democracies been consolidated in Africa? Botswana and Mauritius stand out easily as the two most consolidated democracies in Africa. Against the background of an African average democracy scores of 2.5 in 1980 and 3.3 in 1990, Botswana scores 5.5 in 1980 and 6.5 in 1990. Its high score in 1980 is maintained and further increased by 1 over the ten year period (see table 4.3). Mauritius, which had the highest democracy score of 6.0 in 1980, maintains its score in 1990, an indication of a consolidated democracy. Within the ten year period, only these two countries managed to keep high scores consistently.

The two countries, however have achieved consolidated democracies under different circumstancies. While Botswana is culturally homogenous, Mauritius is a rainbow of cultures in terms of languages, ethnicity and religion. Botswana is on the mainland of Africa while Mauritius is one of the African islands. They also differ in size, population, and most importantly, the approach to consolidating democracies.

## Notes to Chapter Four

1.    The 1960s witnessed events that are sometimes referred to as Africa's first democratic liberation. More than half of the countries gained their independence from colonialism in that year, putting in place democratic constitutions.

2.    For more on transition theories in general, see O'Donnell and Schmitter, ed. (1986), Share (1987), and Pridham, ed. (1991).

3.    Founding-fathers include Kwame Nkrumah of Ghana, Jomo Kenyatta of Kenya, Kenneth Kaunda of Zambia, Julius Nyerere of Tanzania and Houphet Boigny of Cote d'Ivoire. Almost all founding-fathers, with a few exceptions, rule till they die or are forced out of office.

4.    The delayed effect of socio-economic hardships has been explained by Davies's theory of relative deprivation in chapter one.

5.    See also Seligman (1994), and Cohen and Arato (1994).

## Questions to Chapter Four

1. Describe the different types of Transition?

   o Bottom up

   o Top Down

2. Describe the various phases of the two Transition types?

   | Bottom up | Top Down |
   |---|---|
   | Decomposition | Decomposition |
   | Protests | Protests |
   | Election | Liberalization |
   | | Election |

3. Define Civil Society and explain how it influences demo-cratic development?

   " Well informed Society "

## CHAPTER FIVE

# GHANA

## Political History

Richard Rathbone (1994, p. 163) describes Ghana as "... always bewilderingly capable of doing unpredictable things and of doing them before anyone else." Ghana is the first Sub-Saharan African country to attain independence; it was black Africa's first parliamentary government, as well as black Africa's first transition from military back to parliamentary government (David Austin, 1979). It has also set bad examples such as having one of the highest rates of military coups on the continent.[1]

## Political History

Ghana recently moved from an authoritarian military rule to a democracy. The current political system may be described as a form of Guided Democracy because even though Ghana has a democratic constitution, remnants of authoritarian behaviour still exist. The 1992 elections recorded 58% of the votes for Jerry Rawlings, the former authoritarian leader enabling him to become the President of the fourth Republic of Ghana.

Ghana enjoyed a competitive election in 1952, supervised by the then colonial power, which elected Kwame Nkrumah, the first Ghanaian head of government.[2] Since the overthrow of Nkrumah's government in 1966, Ghana came under military control in 1966–1969, 1972–1979, and 1981–1992. In between the military regimes, the country enjoyed democratic governance from 1969–1972, and 1979–1981. The current democratic government, voted in on the first week of November 1992, will go to the polls again in November 1996, as stipulated under the Fourth Republic Constitution (Arthur Banks ed., 1996).

The current Constitution makes use of certain aspects of all four previous ones. It was drafted by a consultative assembly which represented all identifiable groups in the Ghanaian society; groups that include the professional bodies, traditional leaders (Chiefs), women and minority ethnic groups. It was a conscious effort at increasing the social base of political participation.

The constitution dictates a multi-party system as the basis for political competition, with a directly elected president and an appointed vice president, a military-civilian Security Council, a non-partisan Council of State (which plays a mediation role as it is done by respected opinion leaders in most traditional political systems), a unicameral elected legislative body, and a special committee on human rights and administrative justice (Banks ed., 1996). The Consultative Council retained the strengths of the previous constitutions, which has been criticized as too Western (Youry Petchenkine, 1993); they also went to extra lengths to include some indigenous democratic practices (Constitution of Ghana, 1992).

Respect for elders in society for instance, is a strong feature of most Akan socio-political traditions. It is a system where much weight is given to the views of elders in a community because of the notion that, with age comes experience and wisdom. The creation of the institution of Council of State and the criteria for its membership (loosely based on age and accomplishment), is meant to reflect the ideals of this *Elder Respect system.*

The institution of Chieftaincy is one tradition that has refused to die in modern Ghana. There have been many attempts in Ghana's political history to strangle this institution. During the period of establishing colonial authority upon the indigenous people of Ghana, there were many battles fought by the colonial army to strip the political powers of Chiefs. There were the Chiefs who were bought over to recognize the colonial authority, in the process committing political suicide in the eyes of the people because they gave away their authority. There were those who were considered too dangerous to the colonial project, and therefore, had to be physically removed from their areas of authority. The Ashantis, for instance, bore the brunt of the British colonial army in many encounters. Finally, the Ashantehene Nana Prempeh (1) had to be exiled to the Seychelles Island to break the spirit of the Ashantis and the political power of the institution of Chieftaincy (Joseph Dupuis, 1966).[3]

The assault on this august institution was continued even after independence from colonialism. Nkrumah's government, when confronted with the power of the institution of Chieftaincy and the loyalty it still commanded among the people, tried to use both legal and extra legal means to reduce its political significance. New chiefs without any claim to royal lineages were created and recognized by the government, who aimed to reduce the influence of powerful chiefs considered by the government to be their enemies. The institution, in spite of all these efforts has remained strong and continues it's influence in the modern political set up. It is to the credit therefore, of the latest constitution drafters, that the role of the institution of Chieftaincy has been recognized and accorded a significant place in the new democratic system.

To an extent, the current document marries aspects of the British, American and French basic laws (Western philosophy of government), with indigenous Ghanaian social norms and rules. The Fourth Republic Constitution makes conscious efforts to address some of the major criticisms of the past constitutions, notably the insensitivity to traditional authority structures, norms and institutions. It is also sensitive to the frustrations of minority groups, which are mostly created by their disproportional share of socio-economic benefits.

## Transitional Conditions

In most African countries, the condemnation of authoritarianism and the subsequent demand for constitutional rule in the late 1980s had socio-economic frustration as the underlying factor. As has been stated in an earlier chapter, such demands reached a crescendo at a time when the socio-economic conditions were improving because the tolerance level of the people had been reduced to lower limits than the period of the worst socio-economic conditions.

Ghana loosely fits this pattern, even though the decision to give in to the advocates for constitutional rule goes beyond socio-economic conditions. *The Provisional National Defence Council* (PNDC), unlike most African authoritarian regimes was not forced out of office mainly because of dramatic economic and political failures.

By 1991, when Jerry Rawlings formally announced to the nation that the PNDC is now embarking on a program to return the country to a new constitutional order, the successes of its *Economic Recovery Program (ERP)* had been proclaimed by the International economic community, with the IMF vigorously advertising Ghana as a success story of the its recommended Structural Adjustment Program (SAP).[5] In spite of this economic achievement the transition was not a grant from the PNDC. The contention is that because the PNDC had successfully abated the early 1980 economic crisis, it was therefore under no severe pressure to relinquish political power which it had forcibly seized from the constitutionally elected government led by the Peoples' National Party on December, 1981 (see E. Gyimah-Boadi, 1991). What then, pressed the PNDC to agree to a transition to democracy?

By the late 1980s, Ghanaians had begun to feel the hardships of the SAP. The honeymoon of IMF loans and grants was over and Ghana had entered that stage of the ERP where it had no alternative but to start reducing the size of the public sector, stop substantial subsidies given to most parastatal corporations, and eliminate many social programs. By 1985, trade liberalization policies had flooded the markets with hitherto unavailable goods, but the prices were mostly beyond the pockets of the ordinary man and woman in the street.

The cost of living had started to rise, certainly not to the levels of the later years of the 1970s, but the gradual rise was enough to cause concern (see figure 5.1). Expectations had risen prportionately with the constant praises showered on the PNDC's economic policies by the international financial community. Disenchantment began to foster among government workers in particular, and the population in general. Withholding of services for better conditions of service by government employees (mostly a demand for wage increase) became the order of the day. *The Ghana Medical Association, University Teachers Association of Ghana,* and *The Civil Servants Association,* were among the many professional organizations that besieged the government for better remuneration to meet the rising cost of living. The tolerance of the people had gone down considerably, while the demands for a more humane SAP became bolder. The authoritarian style with which the PNDC implemented most of its bitter policies increasingly came under attack during this period. Advocates for democracy were also helped by other factors such as the existence of many social organizations.

## Figure 5.1
### CONSUMER PRCE TREND IN GHANA

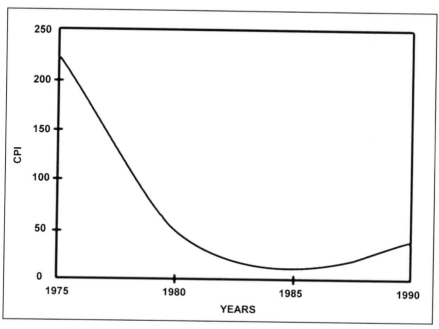

Source: IMF Statistics, 1970, 1980, 1990.

Ghana has enjoyed a vibrant associational life with many of its social and professional organizations functioning as political parties in disguise during the PNDC era when party politics was banned. In spite of alleged ruthless clamp down on members, many of these organizations had consistently throughout the PNDC era, challenged the legitimacy of the military junta (Gyimah-Boadi, 1991).

Private associations such as the Danquah/Busia Heritage had, from time to time, through public lectures, accused the government of incompetence and mismanagement of national programs. The J. B. Danquah Memorial Lectures in 1990 delivered by Professor Adu Boahene for instance, an annual academic exercise, turned out to be a scathing attack on the military regime's dismantling of the educational system.[6] This attack was followed by the public questioning of the PNDC educational system by Professor Akilagpa Sawyerr (the then Vice Chancellor of the University of Ghana), piling up the pressure of the Ghanaian elites on Rawlings and his military junta. These attacks may have been on specific policies, but they generally questioned the legitimacy of an authoritarian regime which did not debate public policies before implementing them.

The private press made their contribution to the efforts at putting pressure on the PNDC in the immediate pre-transition era. In spite of the proscription of many independent newspapers which were critical of the PNDC in its early years, and the physical threat to "unfriendly" journalists, many other newspapers appeared on the newsstands and gradually took bolder stands against the dictatorial rule of the PNDC. *The Christian Chronicle, Leisure, The Gossip, and Young and Old,* continued the work of the banned *Legon Observer, Catholic Standard, and the Pioneer* (Gyimah-Boadi, 1991). There was a sustained onslaught on the legitimacy of the PNDC regime.

In spite of the seemingly insignificant increase in the cost of living, socio-economic conditions became the platform on which the attack on the authoritarian political system was launched. The relative economic success of the PNDC regime could not dilute the potency of political grievances. The elites, having protested the usurpation of power by the military, albeit under the cover of academic and professional organizations, became emboldened by the relative successes in Benin, Zambia, Cape Verde and others on the continent, as well as the crumble of authoritarian rule in Eastern Europe. At this juncture, the PNDC had lost the moral will to keep hanging on to power, and being prodded gently by international trends, wisely decided to give in to a transition to democracy.

## The Transition Style

Ghana's current transition was negotiated among the political and military elites of the country. The PNDC executed a Top-Down type of transition. It was heavily managed. The PNDC

> ... packed the transition process with pro-government organizations and individuals, refusing to place the program in the hands of an independent body (Gyimah-Boadi 1991).

The incumbent refused to relinquish power totally and managed to extract many concessions, as it usually occurs under Top-Down transitions. The initial stages of the transition process did not involve the majority of the citizenry as was the case for instance, in the Zambian transition. With the exception of the referendum which decisively favored a multi-party political system, the critical aspects of the transition was negotiated between the PNDC leaders and the Opposition elites.

The limited role assigned to grassroots movements, on the surface, cast doubts on the intentions of the incumbent, and on the endurance of the political system itself. It feeds the notion that what has taken place in Ghana is not true democracy, but a mockery. The contestation of the election results by the opposition (see Stolen Verdict 1992) and the consequent boycott of the Parliamentary elections tainted the credibility of the transition. But Top-Down transitions do not come with an appreciable level of democraticgains, initially. Its blossom into a full-fledged democracy is gradual, vestiges of authoritarianism are phased out with the growth of the political system. What are Ghana's chances for democratic consolidation? Can the small gains flourish into a full democracy? Will the relative socio-economic gains achieved under the PNDC help sustain democracy?

## Prospects for Consolidation

The current political system in Ghana, as has been stated at the onset, fits the Guided Democracy model. Individual rights and interests are protected, but they must conform to the perceived interest of the state. The state still plays a big role, and the definition of the common interest of the people falls in the lap of the political elites.

Ghana is making efforts to move towards a liberal democracy model. Capitalism is vigorously being pursued. The ruling party for instance, has privatization as the backbone of its efforts to re-vitalize the economy. There is a massive drive to sell off most of the public corporations that have been a financial burden on the government (see for instance, West Africa, 26 February–3 March 1996, pp. 309–312).

In spite of the limited degree of democratic gains, there are many factors in Ghana that favor democratic consolidation. The Top-Down transition style has given elites a lot of control, which is essential in the efforts towards implementing necessary but unpopular policies. Such control is needed in the early stages of an infant democracy. However, efforts continue to be made in the form of decentralizing legislative processes to give the district councils more autonomy in the management of their affairs. This will encourage more grassroots participation in politics, a policy started by the PNDC regime for a totally different reason.[7]

*Economic Recovery.* Economic development seems to be one of the key variables that facilitate democratic consolidation (Adam Przeworski et al., 1996). The ruling Party (NDC), which is an offshoot of the authoritarian Provisional National Defence Council (PNDC) still basks in the glory of having been able to resuscitate the Ghanaian economy from its low-point in the early 1980s. By 1981 for instance, the real GDP had fallen by 15 percent (Donald Rothchild and E. Gyimah-Boadi, 1986). The PNDC, enjoying the advantages of ruling by decrees, designed and implemented many economic recovery programs that were harsh on the people in the short run, but good for the national economy in the long run.

Ghana remains one of the few Third World countries where the implementation of the IMF backed Structural Adjustment Program is touted as successful, both by the ruling government and the international financial community. The economy has registered and maintained a consistent 5% growth rate, a far departure from the negative growth rates that Ghana experienced in the early 1980s (World Bank Report, 1989).

But the Ghanaian economy still has serious problems (see Herbert H. Werlin, 1994). The benefits of the economic success for instance, has not trickled down into the lower classes. Income gaps are still wide. Higher-placed individuals and elite groups have certainly benefited more from the economic growth than the ordinary people who form the majority of the population. The hardships brought about by the attempts to transform the economy from a state-shackled entity to one dominated by the private sector have had severe adverse effects on the ordinary workers (Richard Jeffries, 1991). The PNDC, not having to answer to any electorate during its reign, managed to institute policies that were harsh on the people in the short run but good for the economy in the long run. Currency devaluation for instance, one of the most sensitive issues that has been responsible for overthrow of governments in Ghana, was boldly introduced by the PNDC to bolster the export drive of the Ghanaian economy.

The PNDC, supported by the IMF laid a good economic foundation for the civilian government. Policies were introduced for instance, to cushion the harshness of the Structural Adjustment Program during the liberalization stage. One such effort, *Program of Action to Mitigate the Social Cost of Adjustment* (PAMSCAD) disburses funds and offers job re-training opportunities to those who lost their jobs through the ERA.

The Ghanian economy, with all the shortcomings, has been oriented in the right direction before the new government took office. The economy is being managed to rely more on market mechanisms (Jeffrey Herbst, 1993). There has been a positive response in the government's export drive program, both in the traditional and non-traditional export sectors. The volume of non-traditional export has increased significantly. There has been a reduction in the size and functions of the civil service. Privatization policies have been pursued vigorously, with the government eliminating many of the wasteful state corporations and marketing boards. Most of the economic indicators are moving in the right direction. Ghana's Gross Domestic Product (GDP) during 1984–1988 experienced a steady 6 to 7 percent growth rate (*New York Times*, January 3, 1988. p. 1), making it one of the highest in sub-Saharan Africa. The private sector is expected to become stronger leading the way towards a more robust economic growth. The legitimacy of the political system will increase in such an environment, increasing the chances of democratic consolidation.

*Leadership.* The departure of Kwame Nkrumah from Ghanaian politics left a big leadership gap. Since then, almost all political leaders have been compared to this political stalwart and found wanting. Jerry Rawlings' early years in office may come close to that of Nkrumah, in terms of charisma and the skill at mobilizing grassroots support for political participation. Rawlings has Nkrumah's knack for inspiring followers, and for attracting devotion and enthusiasm. Post-independent Africa has become susceptible to leadership with such qualities, and Rawlings used that to his advantage. Michael Tidy and Ali Mazrui (1991, p. 190) write:

> Charismatic, as distinct from bureaucratic leadership
> has been a marked feature of the style of African po-
> litical leaders both in the nationalist struggle and af-
> ter independence.

Rawlings' eloquence, seeming care for the plight of the ordinary man and woman, his populist style, and his effective control over the security forces helped him to push through a

lot of sound but bitter programs for the upliftment of the national economy. Many leaders would not have survived after
introducing for instance, policies that devalued the *cedi*, reduced the public service and created massive unemployment in
the short run.[8]

Ghana's infant democracy is in a stronger position than
most other new democracies on the continent because Rawlings PNDC government managed to implement many of the bitter but necessary policies. The future of Ghana's democracy to
some extent, will depend on how Rawlings continues his policies, but this time under a more transparent and accountable
system.

*Institutions.* Ghana's fourth Republic constitution attempts to broaden the base for political participation, cater for
the needs of minorities, and make use of some of the traditions
of the people. Multi-party politics, in spite of its competitive nature, is being relied on to bring people of different ethnic, religious, and class persuasion together.

The Constitution recognizes the potential for a political
party to be used as a vehicle for parochial sectoral interests,
especially along ethnic and religious lines. Provisions have
therefore been made to forestall any such intentions. Number 4
of Section 55 of the constitution insists that all political parties
have a national character, and that membership shall not be
based on ethnic, religious, regional or other sectional divisions.
Number 9 insists that members of the national executive
should be chosen from all regions of the country (The Constitution of Ghana, 1992). Sectoral conflicts are minefields to democratic governance and the constitution goes to extra lengths
to avoid its occurrence.

Multi-party politics convention in Ghana encourages a
judicious selection of presidential candidates. In the previous
constitutional regime, most parties were very sensitive to the
ethnic background of their presidential teams. A presidential
candidate from a minority ethnic group with a running mate
from a majority ethnic group seem to be the winning formula
up to date. It worked for the Peoples' National Party (PNP) under Hilla Limann and Joe deGraft-Johnson, and it has worked

for the NDC, with the Ewe (minority) teaming up successfully with the Fanti (Akan majority). Such ethnic coalitions through personal representatives, have augured well for inter-ethnic relations under multi-party politics.

Certain traditions are held in high esteem in Ghana. The change of name upon independence, from the Gold Coast to Ghana (an old West African empire) for instance, attests to the pride Ghanaians attach to traditions. The institution of Chieftaincy and the Elder Respect system are two of such traditions. The empowerment of the National House of Chiefs, and the establishment of the Council of State seem to be a response to the political pull of tradition. Such symbolism in the constitution, as politically weak as they may seem, provides an important bridge between tradition and modernity, avoiding some of the alienation felt by some traditionalists.

*External Support.* The international community has been extremely supportive of Ghana under Rawlings. For a number of reasons, the international image of Ghana under Rawlings (even during the authoritarian era) became rehabilitated. It was a far cry from the late 1970s when Ghana repudiated its foreign debt obligations and became a pariah among the international financial community.

The late 1980s and early 1990s brought in a lot of financial aid to Ghana when its economic program was underwritten by the IMF. Between 1983 and 1988 alone, the IMF committed a total of about $700 million dollars to Ghana's Economic Recovery Program (IMF and World Bank Annual Reports, 1983–1989). Ghana had turned its image around and there is talk about replicating Ghana's structural adjustment success in other African countries (Donald Rothchild, 1991).

Culturally, Ghana has regained the privileged position it occupied among people of African descent in the diaspora, under the charismatic leadership of Kwame Nkrumah. Revenue from the tourism industry has gone up in current years mainly because of the renewed interest in Ghana, of people of African descent in Europe and the Americas. An international festival (Panafest) for instance, was organized recently in Ghana by Africans from all walks of life, in conjunction with the Government of Ghana. President Rawlings and his wife were just honored with doctorate degrees from Lincoln University in the United States of America. This image-booster has influenced the politics of Ghana in two main ways.

First, Rawlings finds himself under pressure to either play a leading role in the drive towards democracy in Africa, in line with the international trend. If Ghana is to continue to enjoy the favors of the international community, then Rawlings has to do away all the remnants of authoritative tendencies to conform with the global democratic trend. With Ghana's Transition being watched critically both within Africa and beyond, Rawlings has no choice but to continue to adhere to the dictates of the constitution, if he values the good image he has created.

Second, the underwriting of Ghana's economy program has a multiplier effect. Expectations have been raised in Ghana, and the current regime is being kept on its toes to deliver the economic goods, but within a politically democratic system. The rejection of the 1996 Value Added Tax (VAT) system through massive demonstrations by people from all political persuasions sent signals to the ruling government that the days when authoritarian means were employed to impose policies were over.

On the other hand, the international community, especially the World Bank's credibility has come to depend on the performance of Ghana's Structural Adjustment Program; they will have to continue to back Ghana's economic and political transition to retain the credibility of their SAP. Ghana and the International Financial Community have created a symbiotic relationship; Ghana has to deliver in terms of democratic governance and economic development, while the West has to continue its support for Ghana to make its development philosophy credible to the rest of the developing world.

## Conclusion

Ghana's transition to democracy was influenced by many factors. The tailing off of the economic growth, the unequal distribution of the socio-economic benefits, and the gradual rise in consumer prices strengthened the voices of the internal pro-democracy advocates to demand a return to constitutional rule. The desire of Ghana to retain the favorable image abroad also softened the resolve of the PNDC to hang on to power. The willingness of the international donors to apply the political conditionality string to its loans influenced the PNDC regime to some extent, to negotiate a transition.

Ghana's transition is of the Top-Down style, with the various elite groups negotiating among themselves about the transition schedule. The incumbent managed to extract many concessions, especially the late insertion of the controversial transition provisions, which denies or questions any activities of the dissolved PNDC and its appointees. While Ghana's transition to democracy was more of a managed exercise, it has the necessary linchpins for consolidation.

The economy has a stronger foundation than many of the its African counterparts that underwent similar transitions. The popularity of Rawlings, and the opportunity given him by the voters to continue the economic recovery program stand democratic consolidation in a good stead. The vibrant opposition leaders have already demonstrated their readiness to press the executive for more political participation and accountability. Consolidation, to a large extent will depend on the level of commitment of the leadership and the elites of democratic governance, and the extent of external support and pressure on the country to remain democratic.

## Notes to Chapter Five

1.   Ghana's first coup came in 1966 when Nkrumah's government was removed when he was on a trip to broker peace in Hanoi. Since then, the county has swung between military regimes and constitutional government.

2. Ghana was named the Gold Coast by the British because of its abundant gold resource. The adpoted name of Ghana belongs to an ancient West African empire.

3. Ashantis dominated territorially and in military might and therefore presented the most formidable opposition to colonial expansion.

4. In Ghana, the King or Chief sits on a Stool and not a Throne.

5. The announcement was splashed in the front pages of all major newspapers, especially The Daily Graphic, and The Ghanaian Times.

6. Adu Boahene's bold public criticism of the PNDC catapulted him to be the leading opponent of Rawlings. He came second in the transition elections and is currently the leader of the opposition.

7. Empowering the district councils was Rawlings strategy to dilute the power of the political elites of Ghanaian politics.

8. Cedi is the national currency of Ghana.

# Questions to Chapter 5

1. What efforts were made in the current Constitution to increase the participation base in Ghana?

2. What are the factors that facilitate democratic consolidation in Ghana?

## CHAPTER SIX

# ZAMBIA

## Political History

Zambia, which used to be Northern Rhodesia became independent from British colonial rule in 1964. The fight for independence was led by Kenneth Kaunda and Harry Nkumbula. Kaunda's party, United National Independence Party (UNIP), won the first democratic elections in 1964 and formed the first national government, with Nkumbula's African National Congress (ANC) as the Opposition party. Kaunda's re-election in 1968 for another four year term emphasized his dominance in this new nation, encouraging him to introduce a one-party state in 1972. This act, set the stage for almost three decades of personal rule (Stephen Chan, 1992).

In August 1991, the National Assembly under Kaunda's leadership, having come under severe internal and external pressure, was pressed to approve and sign a multi-party constitution. A couple of months later, national elections were held for a presidential and parliamentary seats under the supervision of international observers including the United Nations Team and a non-governmental group led by President Jimmy Carter. Frederick Chiluba won 74 percent of the presidential vote against Kaunda, while his Movement for Multiparty Democracy (MMD) captured 125 of the 150 Assembly seats (Banks ed., 1996).

Until the adoption of multi-party elections in 1991, Zambia had been under a one-party, presidential-parliamentary system. Kaunda was the sole presidential candidate and the result of those one-sided elections was expected. For instance, the 1983 and 1988 presidential elections reported an overwhelming 93 percent and 96 percent votes respectively, in favor of President Kaunda.

Zambian politics at this point was as monolithic as its economy. Hardly any line existed between the government and party structures. UNIP became the sole agent of distribution of national services. Keith Panter-Brick (1994, p. 236) writes:

> This was particularly true at the local level where the right to elect the district council had passed from the electorate to the party. From top to bottom the administration had been infiltrated so that services were provided, regulations issued and benefits conferred by persons acting on the party's behalf rather than in the name of the state.

Kaunda became accountable to no one, and he used the institutionalized "state of emergency" to cripple and silence public opposition to his rule. The Kaunda regime became discredited and could not provide any form of good governance (Munyonzwe Hamalengwa, 1992). When the International financial community refused to continue bank-rolling the inevitable inefficiencies, the die was cast for the collapse of the regime from the weight of the mounting internal and external debts (Jean M. Due, 1993).

Internal pressures, mounted mostly by the poverty-stricken population, included members of the Zambian Congress of Trade Unions (ZCTU) Changes were demanded from Kaunda. The National Assembly in 1991, adopted a new constitution that abolished the one-party system in favor of a multiparty democracy. They also adopted a two-tiered parliament, and replaced the post of prime minister with a vice-presidency. The cabinet was to owe its appointment to the president (Banks ed., 1996). Surprisingly, the presidential power to impose a state of emergency, a clause which impedes the attainment of democracy was retained. They only reduced the length of time it could be imposed from sixth months to three months. Ironically, this instrument which was a major source of vexation to the MMD during the electioneering campaigns was to be used by the Chiluba government after the transition to democracy.

## Transitional Conditions

No single event can explain sufficiently the demise of Kaunda and his one-party system, but the 1986 rioting and looting by Zambians (when food subsidies were removed), comes close to being the most impacting of all the problems the government faced. This incident was a result of years of accumulated debt, withdrawal of international financial aid, economic mis-management, and political ineptitude.

In the early 1980s, the booming copper industry enabled Zambians to enjoy one of Africa's highest standards of living. Zambia is the world's sixth leading producer of copper. In addition to copper which accounts for 80–95 percent of the country's exports, the country is rich in other minerals including cobalt, zinc, coal, and sulphur (Banks ed., 1996). By 1985, Zambia had enjoyed special treatment from the IMF more than any other sub-Saharan African country. Its borrowings from the IMF in 1983 for instance, was 235 percent of its quota (Kenneth Good 1989).

The decline in copper prices during the mid 1980s exposed the inefficiencies in the economy. The economy's dependence on one major product made it vulnerable to the turbulence of mid-1980 international economic crisis. Soon the country's internal and external debt became unbearable to manage. Internally, state institutions had accrued huge debts. Kenneth Good (1989) provides a summary of Zambia's indebtedness at this period. The Zambian Airways Corporation owed the Department of Aviation more than 1 million *kwacha* (the Zambian currency) in air revenue. Zambia Railways had been unable to collect the 30 million kwacha owed it by other state corporations. The United Bus Company was in serious debt to the tune of 50 million kwacha. The University of Zambia's teaching hospital owed Medical Stores Ltd. more than 8 million kwacha. The Banks and Mining Corporations were not faring any better. The Zambian National Bank had given bad loans, the disclosing of which was politically unsafe at the time. Its holding company, Zambia Industrial and Mining Corporation

(Zimco) was running itself into the ground because of huge debts.

The external debt had mounted to about $6 billion within a remarkably short time (Banks ed., 1994). When the country failed to meet its services and interests obligations on the debt, its access to the coffers of the international financial community was blocked, starting a sharp decline in the standard of living. Zambians began to experience severe socio-economic frustrations. The cost of living became unbearable around 1986 when the government, under the pressure from the international financial community (especially the IMF), removed subsidies in the agricultural sector. This move affected almost everybody, but most harshly the ordinary people due to the steep 120 percent increase in the prices of food, including the staple maize meal (Peter Burnell, 1994).

The rioting that broke out as a result of this increase in the cost of living sounded the dying bells of the one-party system. Kaunda had refused over the years to heed to the protests of Zambians. He had blamed external sources for Zambia's problems in the process, succeeding in holding on to his authoritarian regime (*The Economist*, November 20, 1993, p. 47). He tried to ward off the imminent by re-instating the subsidies to buy off the demands for political change. The pressure for a political change increased and Kaunda stuck to his guns, hoping to stifle it as he had done so many times during his thirty year rule. Finally in 1990, when the regime came close to being overthrown by a military coup, Kaunda realized it was time to accept a multi-party system of governance in Zambia. A multi-party system was then proposed and endorsed in October 1991.

Unlike Ghana, Zambia's transition was forced out of the ruling government due to socio-economic hardships. The suffocating impact of a leadership that had outlived its good days, a corrupt party that erased all lines between it and the government, and an economy that had severely been mismanaged combined with the de-stabilization activities of the South African Defence Force to bring about a dramatic transition to democracy.

The cost of living climbed very high in the mid 1970s. By early 1980s, prices had fallen very steeply, allowing Zambians to enjoy a relatively comfortable life. However, by 1986 when the riots broke out, the cost of living had started rising as sharply as it has fallen, creating a difficult socio-economic environment in a relatively short time (John Mukela, 1987). Zambians started questioning Kaunda's governing philosophy more seriously.

By 1988, in an attempt to ward off demands for political change, Kaunda introduced economic reform measures, attracting much-needed foreign exchange from the international financial community. Food subsidies for instance, were restored. Zambians at this point rather increased their demands for political reforms, culminating finally in the October 1991 announcement of plans for a transition to multi-party system of governance. Conforming to the general pattern in Africa, the transition took place not in the mid 1970s when socio-economic hardships were at its worst. The reprieve in the early 1980s reduced the tolerance level and increased the expectations of the people. Even though the mid 1980s conditions were not as harsh as the 1970s, demands for political reforms increased, forcing the transition to democracy in the 1990s (see figure 5.2 for an illustration). The transition, however, is different from what occurred in Ghana.

## The Transition Style

Zambia experienced a bottom-up transition, unlike Ghana due to a number of reasons. First, the mismanaged economic system had created a great gap between the tiny wealthy elite and the rest of the population which could barely make ends meet. While gaps between social classes is not unique in both Western and Third World societies, the economic differences between the mostly political elites and the rest of the population in Zambia is despairingly wider. Good (1989) documents the gap between the classes. In the late 1970s, the lowest fifth of households received only 3.4 percent of the national income, while the highest fifth reserved 61.1 percent for itself.

Neighboring Malawi, by no means a wealthier country had a comparable elites to masses ratio of 10.4 to 50.6. The Zambian ratio worsened around 1985 when the elite's share further increased by 50 percent, at a time when the average real wages were falling by 40 percent. Good (p. 309) states:

> the increasing wealth of a small minority in Zambia has been accompanied by the impoverishment, steepening in recent years, of the great majority, without the domestic accumulation which might justify inequalities in a developing capitalist system.

The wide unhealthy economic gap between the elites and the masses also created a gap of distrust between them, making it difficult for a Top-Down transition to take place. Without the people trusting the elites, not much room for elite negotiations was left, especially so when the demands for change had essentially been orchestrated by the people.

## Figure 5.2
## CONSUMER PRICE TREND IN ZAMBIA

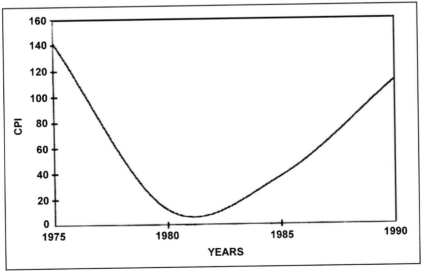

Source: IMF Statistical YearBook

Zambia's recent political history also favored a Bottom-Up transition. Southern African countries, unlike their West African counterparts wrenched their independence from the colonial powers through some degree of armed struggle. This factor encouraged the creation of mass organizations to fight against the colonial power. Zambia's experience in mass organizations was bolstered by the need created by continued attacks on the country from the apartheid South Africa, even after independence had been granted by the British.

The positive side of such an experience was strong national unity under a leadership seen as a father of the nation. On the negative side, it discouraged a full growth of different interest groups, with the exception of those along ethnic divisions. Finally, when the political situation in Zambia came to a head and a change was demanded, the mass movement experience came readily in hand, hence the bottom-up approach.

The Zambia transition was not as managed as Ghana's. Kaunda was defeated by a rapid series of events that surprised him and many political analysts. He initially refused any reforms and blamed most problems on the international financial community, a tactic that had worked for him for most part of his rule (*The Economist*, November 20, 1993). Spontaneous riots broke out against his mis-rule, followed immediately by an unsuccessful coup attempt, Kaunda had to allow a transition in a rushed manner. When a multi-party system was finally announced, Kaunda had lost the control over the political developments that were taking place. He had to swim with the events and hope that he remained at the helm of it all when things settled.

While Ghana's transition was very much controlled by Rawlings with little pushes from the pro-democracy advocates, Zambia's transition pace was dictated mostly by a loose association of the Christian Churches and other mass organizations. Zambia has a sizeable Christian population and the pulpit in this instance was effectively used as a platform for political reforms. Religion, far from becoming the opium of the masses, became the focal point for political transformation.[1]

As had been argued earlier on, Bottom-Up transitions are characterized by broad-based participation. Zambia's transitional process was more broad-based than Ghana's, the big difference being in democratic gains after the initial transition (see tables 4.2 and 4.3). The drama surrounding the political transformation awakened many dormant organizations.[2] Many organizations sprung up and volunteered to monitor the elections, ensuring full participation at the grassroot level. In 1991, six Zambian civic organizations came together to form the *Zambia Elections Monitoring Coordinating Committee* (ZEMCC). The organizations include the Christian Churches, the Law Association of Zambia, the National Women's Lobby Group, the Press Association of Zambia, the University of Zambia students' Union, and the NGO Coordinating Committee.

Not surprisingly, the unusually high levels of civic activities exhibited during the election monitoring period had not produced any seasoned political leaders because of the overwhelming dominance of the Kaunda regime. The churches and other organizations lacked political experience and were not a factor in influencing the type of a democratic system that replaced the one-party system. The inertia of a one-party state had robbed Zambians of experienced political leaders. Frederick Chiluba, a Trade Unionist and strong Christian who became the elected President in the new democratic system has been fumbling so far, and his personal performance will be a significant factor in the consolidation of the democratic gains.

## Prospects for Consolidation

Zambia's successful transition encouraged many pro-democracy advocates in Africa because of the seemingly entrenched position of Kaunda and his sound defeat. It proved that entrenched authoritarian leaders, whatever their status and past contribution to their countries, could be defeated and changed peacefully through the ballot box. The mass involvement of the ordinary citizens conforms to the definition of the ideal democracy. Equally creditable is the precedent Zambia set in including foreign observers to monitor the elections, given the checkered history of such elections in sub-Sahara Africa.[3] More importantly, the glorious acceptance of defeat by the incumbent gave hope to many that the rules of the democracy game have started to take roots in Africa.

There are others, however, who call for caution in the interpretation of the political events in Zambia. Panter-Brick (1994) for instance, argues that Zambia's transition was an event determined extraneously, and had little to do with a commitment to democracy in Zambia. He further questions the aspirations of the Chiluba government and the MMD, wondering if they will be any different from "many nationalist movements which were elected to office at the time of decolonization ..." (p 231). In the midst of such different interpretations, what will be the prospect for democratic consolidation? An examination of some of the elements crucial to democratic consolidation will help answer the question.

*Leadership.* Leadership plays an important role in democratic sustenance. Federick Chiluba is at a disadvantaged position because of lack of experience (Jowie Mwiinga, 1994). The long years of partisan one-party rule has inhibited the development of potential democratic leaders. Chiluba who was a candidate from the influential Trade Union Workers of Zambia will need to exhibit extraordinary leadership skills to sustain the democratic gains. He does not have the benefit of continuity that Jerry Rawlings of Ghana has. Rawlings' NDC government retained about 80 percent of his civilian administrators who served under his quasi-military regime. Chiluba's cabinet as well as his political philosophy is totally different from the one he defeated in elections. A totally new beginning on an unfamiliar political road will require tenacity, dedication and support from Zambians and the international community.

Fortunately, the end of apartheid in South Africa means that Zambians will not have to deal will the destabilization activities from across the border; an exercise that immensely taxed the leadership skills of his predecessor. Unfortunately, the support from within has not been forthcoming. One of the major problems of a bottom-up transition is that expectations

of the people once whetted, are difficult to satisfy in the short
run. In his relatively short time in office, Chiluba has had to
resort to the utilization of the State of Emergency powers, a
tool he found vexatious when it was used by Kaunda (Melinda
Ham, 1993).

Kaunda, who consented graciously to defeat amid praise
from opponents, has not been too quiet out of office. His pro-
nouncements and the alleged subversive activities of his immediate family members have put pressure on Chiluba and his
new government. Chiluba lacks the charisma that Rawlings
has. This attribute is essential in the immediate period of transition when the citizens are unsure of the direction of the government. Personal leadership, supported by dedicated elite
groups will be needed in the coming years to retain and further
the march towards democratic consolidation.

*Economic Recovery.* Zambia's faltering economy was the
main reason behind Kaunda's defeat and the transition to democracy. The socio-economic conditions have improved since
then, but it is still a far cry from the years when Zambia enjoyed one of the highest living standards in Africa (Peter
Burnell, 1994). The extent of indebtedness to the international
financial community and the horizontal debts among state
corporations will need astute fiscal management. There is a
pressing need to halt internal economic regression as well as
the decline in international trade (Christopher Adam, 1995).
Externally however, there are two factors that may be favorable
to Zambia's economic well-being.

The international financial community is gradually beginning to reward Zambia's shift to democracy. The country's
credibility has not returned to the 1970 levels but the re-
negotiating efforts to pay its loans is bound to re-open more
widely than before, its access to the needed foreign exchange.
The Trade Unionists from whom Chiluba emerged, favor economic liberalization policies, and the pressure being mounted
on the MMD will ensure some level of economic accountability,
a factor that was concspicously missing in the Kaunda regime.
Lack of accountability, especially among political operatives

caused inimical damage to the economy during the Kaunda years.

The end of apartheid and the emergence of a strong democratic leadership in Nelson Mandela of South Africa will have two positive effects on Zambia's economy. First, the cessation of raids on Zambian economic targets will save the country a lot of human and fiscal resources. The removal of the fear of potential raids will give a psychological boost to the morale of the people and may increase productivity.

The Southern African region stands to benefit from a friendlier economic power next door. There is bound to be more facilitation of trade, not only between Zambia and South Africa, but the region as a whole. *The Southern Africa Development Coordinating Conference* (SADCC), of which Zambia is an active member will grow stronger with the inclusion of South Africa. With the right policies, Zambia stands to reap more benefits from a more peaceful Southern Africa because it has relatively more resources and infrastructure than a lot of its neighbors. A stronger economy under a democracy will not only produce more to share, reducing potential socio-economic protests, but it will also raise the level of the legitimacy of the political system. Higher legitimacy usually means better chances for political stability, an ingredient needed for economic growth.

*Civic Space.* In spite of the inertia of the long one-party rule, a relatively good number of civic organizations sprung up during the transitional period and that made it easier to conduct the elections in a peaceful manner. The existence of women organizations, law associations, national student groups, trade unions and press associations among others, inculcated a sense of civic responsibilities in the population in general. The transfer of social civility into the realm of politics will help democratic consolidation.

The churches in particular were instrumental in the recent transition. The three leading Christian denominations (*the Zambia Episcopal Conference, the Evangelical Fellowship,* and *the Christian Council*) for instance, formed a coalition to help in the smooth conduct of the elections. A conscious harnessing and development of this civic virtue in the population by the government will help the consolidation effort.

## Conclusion

Zambia's transition, initiated by severe deteriotion in the standard of living, was essentially mass-led. The depth of the socio-economic gap between the small elites and the rest of the population influenced the nature of the transition; a Bottom-Up approach that saw a much broader grassroot participation than the Ghanaian transition.

One of the main conditions that favor democratic consolidation in Zambia is the level of its civic activities. Voluntary organizations have been given a new life and this will help sustain the democratic environment that the transition has created. But there remain serious obstacles to democratic consolidation.

Chiluba inherited a severely damaged economy. In the long run, a continued decline will be the biggest hurdle for democratic consolidation. Chiluba received a favorable nod in 1994 from Western donors for his economic policies, and a $300 million aid package that was suspended in 1993 has been restored (Good, 1992).[4] Drastic measures along the lines taken by Rawlings of Ghana under the PNDC regime which managed to slash inflation rates and liberalize the hitherto excessively state controlled economy will be needed in Zambia. But the problem of massive corruption remains, and dissension within his party is eroding party unity (Jowie Mwiinga, 1994). There is unease in his party, causing resignations of some key ministers. The immediate problem is how to further the economic cause to maintain the confidence of the international financial community. Chiluba will also have to convince the population to accept the current socio-economic frustrations as temporarily, and rid his party of corrupt elements to continue to enjoy the massive support needed for successful policy implementation. Ghana under Rawlings has managed this problem successfully so far. Zambia will need to do the same to enhance its prospects for consolidation.

# Notes to Chapter Six

1. Karl Marx in the Communist Manifesto, describes religion as the opium of the masses because of its alleged intoxicating effect on the people. He argues that religion blindfolds the poor, preventing them from rising up against exploitation.

2. Kaunda's repressive regime, against the expectations of classical authoritarian pattern could not stifle the formation of civic organizations. The unity needed in fighting against South African aggression, even after independence may explain this exception.

3. For more on Zambia's elections, see Eric Bjornlund, Michael Bratton and Clark Gibson, 1992.

4. For more on Zambia's fiscal policies, see Christopher Adam, 1995.

## Questions to Chapter Six

1.  Discuss why Zambia experienced the Bottom-Up Transition
    Type?

2.  What are the prospects for consolidation in Zambia?

## CHAPTER SEVEN

# BOTSWANA

## Political History

Botswana, which used to be called Bechuanaland under British protectorate from 1885, became independent in 1966. Since its independence, the country has enjoyed a stable liberal democracy, and has often been referred to as 'a showplace of democracy in Africa' (Banks ed., 1996). Botswana shares a border and interacts with the Republic of South Africa on many economic issues.

Botswana is culturally homogenous, with eight main ethnic groups and a small San population. The Tswana culture dominates the country; John D. Holm and Patrick P. Molutsi estimate that "an overwhelming majority" (around 80 percent) belong to one of the major Twsana ethnic groups. The Setswana language is the first or second language of more than eighty percent of the population.

The modern government has taken advantage of this cultural homogeneity and has adopted assimilative policies to strengthen it further. While government records and radio broadcasts are done only in Tswana languages, non-Tswana languages are allowed for instruction in schools.

Botswana has had another positive advantage in its ethnic relations. The Tswana groups perceive themselves as having equal status in the country and recognize the right of existence of each other. Politics is about perception so this healthy view of the Tswana groups, cultivated by fair political decisions after independence has helped Botswana avoid the destructive ethnic conflicts that have plaqued many African countries.

Since its independence, there have been competitive elections, with the constitution being adhered to, to the letter, a feat not found in many African countries. Botswana has also transformed itself from being one of the poorest countries in

1966, to the one of the fastest growing economies in the world today (Mike Sill, 1993). The discovery of minerals is only part of the story. Many other African countries have precious minerals and other export-earning resources but have not achieved the successes Botswana has. What then accounts for Botswana's political and economic successes?

## Consolidating Conditions

*Economic Policies.* Since independence, Botswana's economy has experienced consistent phenomenal growth. According to Charles Harvey and Stephen R. Lewis, Jr. (1990, p. 1), for the first twenty five years (1965–1985), Botswana had the 'fastest growing economy in the world'. It recorded an 8.3 percent growth of GNP per capita. By 1992, the GNP per capita had reached $2,790, one of the highest in Africa.

Many other areas of the economy have impressive records as well. The ratio of debt service to exports in the 1990s is a mere 4 percent, a very rare statistic in Africa. With prudent fiscal policies, Botswana's economy has been moving in the right direction in many areas of development (see table 6.1).

It is inaccurate to credit this remarkable development solely to the discovery of diamonds (Theodore R. Valentine, 1993). While diamonds remain a formidable foundation to this healthy economy, sound management has been the key to its continued success. Kenneth Good (1992, p. 75) argues that this achievement has been made possible:

> largely through the supportive interrelations between an open market economy and a system of elite democracy, successfully blending 'traditional' and modern elements, and offering a range of fairly free and meaningful political choices.

The Botswana Democratic Party (BDP) operates an efficient market economy with prudent fiscal and monetary policies. Charles Harvey and Stephen Lewis (1990) describe Botswana's economic policies as coherent, capable and meaningful, unlike many other

African economies marked by wasteful and incomplete projects. Christopher Colclough and Stephen McCarthy (1992, p. 75) agree that the economy has benefited immensely from "careful planning, economic management and diplomacy."

The ruling elites of Botswana have been credited with good management and negotiating skills long before the advent of colonialism. Pauline Peters (1983, p. 31) writes about the group leaders of the cattle-men's strong "identity, vitality and power to do things." This particular negotiating skill has served Botswana very well during its dealings with the international financial community. Botswana has managed to secure good deals from various negotiations for mineral exploitation with Trans National Corporations, and also with fellow African neighbors with regards to custom duties. How did Botswana manage to win such favorable concessions from trans-national corporations, an achievement that has eluded many other African countries?

## Table 6.1
### *Highlights of Botswana's Economy*

| | |
|---|---|
| Per capita GDP | $2,300 |
| International Reserves | $3,300 |
| Ratio of Debt Service To Exports | 4% |
| Economic Growth | 5% * |
| Life Expectancy | 60 |

Sources: Kenneth Good (1992), Arthur Banks (1995), and Tom Meisenhelder (1994).

*Leadership Skills.* Batswanan society has always been dominated by elites. In pre-colonial times, the Chief and important Tswana cattle owners were in control of the society. The current political system which depends strongly on elite consensus therefore is a continuation of the pre-independent social structure. The British colonial administration approved the elitist control of the society and teamed up with them, especially the Chiefs to govern the country. The British and the Tswana elites had an inter-dependent relationship; the British had what they wanted without upsetting the social hierarchical structure and in cooperation, the Chiefs and the cattle owners retained their social positions in society (Patrick Molutsi and John D. Holm, 1990).

Transition to independence was relatively smooth because the British not only did they leave the existing social structure intact but they actually encouraged it by contributing to the electoral success of the elitist Botswana Democratic Party (BDP). According to Louis Picard (1987), the European commercial community, prompted by the colonial administration in Botswana made hefty contributions to the coffers of the BDP, giving it a big edge over the other parties.

The favoring of an elite party by departing colonial administration is not unique. Botswana's uniqueness comes from the fact that the elites after independence utilized this power properly in the interest of the whole nation. Seretse Khama, the first president of independent Botswana has been credited with most of Botswana's successes because of his special leadership skills. Good (1992, p. 74) is impressed by the "honesty, pragmatism, and common sense" of both Khama and his successor Quett Masire.

The Botswana leadership has made the right choices for the country and has managed to avoid the mismanagement, the waste, and the political corruption found in neighboring countries. For instance, strong and effective institutions of control have been created to serve as watchdogs of government operations (Diamond, 1988). This unusual high quality management has made the difference between Botswana and many struggling post-independent states.

In spite of the high level of elite consensus, which is the hallmark of the Botwsana political system, there is political competitiveness. The dominance of the ruling BDP has not totally shut out the opposition. The vote percentage of the strongest opposition, the Botswana National Front (BNF) for instance, went up from 20.2 percent in 1984 to 26.9 percent in 1989. It is common for a country doing so well under the ruling party to dominate, but the traditional elite rivalry has kept the modern democracy competitive. Tradition has come to the aid of a modern system. The spirit of competition is maintained because the country relied on some of its traditional institutions which encourage healthy rivalry among ethnic groups and social classes.

*Institutions.* The uniqueness of Botswana's democracy has attracted many different descriptions. It has been characterized by Diamond (1988) as paternalistic, by Good (1992) as elitist, and by Molutsi (1988) as liberal. The proliferation of accolades for this form of democracy stems from the fact that Botswana has blended traditional and Westminster institutions to produce peculiar form of democracy. It is undoubtedly dominated by elites, but it also has fora for grassroots participation.

The dominance of the elites in modern Botswana can be understood by examining the society of pre-colonial and colonial Bechuanaland. Powerful Chiefs and rich cattle owners were always in control before the British took over. Colonial Bechuanaland, before the exploitation of diamonds, was relatively poor and the British therefore decided not to spend too much in the administration of the colony. It utilized its famous 'Indirect Rule' policy where local structures of authority were left intact.[2]

At the height of colonial rule, British administrators and traditional elites shared a common interest, retaining the control and status they wielded in that society. When the time came for independence, as stated already, the British, joined by other rich European expatriates financed the BDP (a group of Tswana elites) to win and retain power in the new Botswana (Good, 1992). The ruling elites however, represent almost all sections of the Botswana society, traditional authorities (the Chiefs), bureaucracy (civil servants), business and farming interests, and the expatriate community (financiers and technocrats of big foreign companies operating in the country).

The concept of elite democracy is (in itself) not unique to Botswana. The Botswana system is different because of two main factors namely the exceptional selflessness of the elites in the effective management of the country's resources and more importantly, the retention of the *Kgotla* system, a traditional forum for grassroot political participation.

In Western societies, one of the major facilitators of democracy is the modern means of communication. The television, newspapers and the radio play key roles in the canvassing of opinions on issues, and also in the dissemination of information about government policies. In African countries, the under-development of modern means of communication, the lack of one national language understood by all, and the high levels of illiteracy rates come together to cripple effective political discussions and participation. Botswana has averted this problem with its retention of, and the introduction of the *Kgotla* and the *Freedom Square* systems.

The Kgotla is a place where the community meets and discusses issues of common interest under the chief's supervision. It provides the people the platform to trade ideas and to come to agreement on government programs that affects the community. It also serves as the forum for collecting views on issues before the government comes out with a policy, affording the people the opportunity to influence government policies before they are enacted. It also has an adjudication role because occasionally, the chief and his advisors deliberate on legal cases involving the members of the community (Molutsi, 1988).[3]

Discussions are conducted freely without fear of repercussions. Criticisms are meted out where due, and not even the Chief is spared under such circumstances. However, traditional ways of behavior are strictly observed. No harsh language is allowed and discipline is enforced immediately when one breaks the traditional observation of decorum.

Such rigid adherence to traditions has sometimes attracted criticisms of censureship. Also, immigrants had been barred from attending kgotla meetings in pre-colonial times. Previously, women and men below a certain age were also not allowed to freely engage in discussions at Kgotla meetings. The modern Kgotla system has sought to remove all these restrictions. In spite of the fact that these barriers have all been eliminated to increase its range of inclusiveness, Kgotla meetings are still relatively restrictive (James J. Zaffiro, 1993). The presence of the Chief can sometimes be intimidating. Kgotla agenda are mostly community based and therefore not many national issues get the chance to be deliberated on. The freedom square system was therefore introduced in the 1960s to improve the range of issues, and also to allow more freedom of speech.

The freedom square system can be equated to the Western political rally concept. It is a political gathering where members of the public and politicians meet to discuss freely issues of national interest without fear of victimization. Unlike the Kgotla meetings, freedom square gatherings do not observe any traditional norms of behavior, and discussions can be based on any issue determined by the gathering. It is a no-hold-barred discussion where partisanship is often the order of the day John Holm and Patrick Molutsi, 1988).

In effect while the Kgotla discusses mostly issues of relevance to a particular ethnic group or community, freedom squares normally take on issues of national dimensions. Kgotla has sometimes been a one-way communication, in that the Chief and the civil servants in charge of the specific program under discussion sometimes overwhelm the community with their expertise and authority. Freedom square discussions, on the other hand, cut across specific issues and goes back and forth, depending on the interests of the gathering. No special status is accorded participants of freedom square gatherings and issues are therefore discussed on equal footing. The two systems put together create the needed opportunity for the ordinary Batswana to be heard directly in political deliberations. These institutions, together with external support have helped raise the levels of legitimacy of the country's democratic system.

*External Influences.* Botswana has attracted the interest of the international community because of its pragmatic economic policies, free market economy, political stability and reasonably good human rights record (Robert L. Curry, Jr., 1986). It has good relations with many Western democracies. The United States of America for instance, has mutual social and economic agreements with Botswana. Botswana for in-stance, has allowed the construction of NASA ground-tracking station and a major Voice of America transmitter on its soil, and in turn receives a relatively good portion of US aid allo-cated to Sub-Saharan Africa.

Its mineral wealth has also attracted active foreign in-volvement in its economy, attracting corporations such as *AMAX* and *ESSO*. Botswana has also been successful in acquiring funding for many of its national programs. A notable one is the *Accelerated Rural Development Program* (ARDP). Such external support has helped in sustaining the high rate of economic growth and political stability. With the interna-tional economic system undergoing major changes because of the end of the cold war, and with South Africa ceasing to be an international pariah, Botwsana will face new challenges in the coming future. Its sustenance will depend on continued skilled leadership, a quality that has served the country well in the past.

## Conclusion

Diamonds and sound fiscal management have propelled Botswana from a poor country immediately after independence to one of Africa's highest per capita income, with an economic growth rate considered to be one of the world's fastest. Relying on a shrewd blend of a tradition which is democratic in es-sence, and some aspects of the Westminster parliamentary system, a unique form of a liberal democracy has been built and sustained.

The economy, however, is coming under some strains (Keith Sommerville, 1994). South Africa is no more the interna-tional pariah because of its recent political transformation and therefore is positioned to compete with Botswana over the at-traction of foreign investment in the region. The dependence on minerals to the exclusion of agricultural development also threatens food security from time to time (Theodore R. Valen-tine, 1993).

A wide gap is developing in income-earning and asset accumulation. The benefits of the economic growth are not trickling down as effectively as it was expected, widening the socio-economic differences between the elites and the rest of the population. Natural calamities such as drought mount occasional assault on the standard of living of the Batswana. These occasional natural threats have serious implications for the stability of the political system.

Botswana's political system is, however, deeply embedded in its time-honored traditions of concern for each other and broad participation in communal issues. These traditions are an asset to modern democracy. The ruling elites have also demonstrated a high sense of consensus and the ability to make the right decisions in the interest of the whole nation. Given the fact that South Africa has now ceased its destabilizing activities, enhancing the development potential of the Southern Africa region, Botswana stands a chance of improving its achievements. The country's chances are brighter because it has already laid the necessary political and economic foundations, compared to its neighbors. A regional economic boom because of the new cooperative South Africa will benefit Botswana more because of its comparative regional advantage.

## Notes to Chapter Seven

1.  Cited in Goran Hyden and Michael Bratton, ed., 1992.

2.  Indirect rule was also applied in many other British colonies, especially in Northern Nigeria.

3.  Cited in Holm and Molutsi, 1988, p. 217.

# Question to Chapter Seven

1. Explain the conditions that contributed to democratic consolidation in Botswana?

## CHAPTER EIGHT

# MAURITIUS

## Political History

Mauritius, a small island in the Indian Ocean formerly known as Ile de France has one of the most stable liberal democracies in Africa (Banks ed. 1996). In a continent that has experienced a lot of political violence because of its plurality, Mauritius has devised and maintained a consociational democracy that has avoided the usual violent conflicts associated plural societies.

Before independence in 1968, this small country had come under the control of many European countries, from the Portuguese through the Dutch, the French and finally the British. Its unique history includes a society, which was about 90 percent slaves or indentured laborers to one which has made an art form of politics of coalitions (Larry W. Bowman, 1991). The success story of Mauritius is not limited to the political arena. There has been a major successful economic transformation as well, from a sugar-dependent economy to a flourishing diversified and industrialized market economy.

The open, export-oriented, market-driven economy has managed to reduce inflation drastically, create an almost unemployment- free society, improve the standard of living and still have a positive balance of payment, all within six years (Richard Kearney, 1991). With a national income per capita of $3,000, an amount much higher than the average national per capita income in Africa (Yang Guilan, 1990), Mauritius has managed to raise itself from a natural resource-less country that could not feed itself, to one with the most impressive socio-economic statistics in Africa (see table 6.2). What makes this miracle more astonishing is that it has been achieved in a society which is divided along every imaginable social fault line, from religious and ethnic cleavages to economic and linguistic divisions. What is the extent of this diversity?

## Table 6.2
### *Highlights of Mauritius' Economy*

| | |
|---|---|
| Per capita GDP | $2,980 |
| Agriculture | 12% |
| Manufacturing | 26.5% |
| Tourism | 5% |
| Exchange Rate of 1 Rupee | $14.45 |
| Life Expectancy | 8 |
| External Debt Service Ratio | 1% |
| Balance of Payment | +MR 1.2 Billion* |

Sources: A.R. Manick (1989), Arthur Banks (1995), L. Bowman (1991).

## Mauritian Society

Mauritius has an extraordinarily diverse society in terms of religions, ethnicity and languages. It is a polyglot of cultures. It has a peculiar history of having no group of people claiming to be the indigenous people of the land; all trace their ancestry to an immigrant past. Over the years, people have come to settle in the country from Europe, Africa, India, and East Asia (Bowman, 1991). Its colonial past exposed it to the rule of the three European powers mentioned before, while slaves and indentured laborers were brought in from Africa and Asia. The end of colonialism and the abolition of slavery produced a free and independent Mauritius with a highly diversified society.

With a current population of slightly over 1 million (Banks ed., 1996), the bulk of the population are of Indian and Pakistani descent, according to Guilan (1990). Europeans and Africans form the next majority, with the Chinese making up the rest of the population (see Table 6.3).

Ethnic identification has received a high degree of attention in relation to finding a durable political system to accommodate a plural society. The Mauritian case becomes even more complicated because the various ethnic groups further maintain different cultural attributes such as language and religion.

Language has particularly become problematic because of its linkage to social and political status. Thomas Hylland Eriksen (1990), has argued that the language situation in Mauritius is much more complex than in virtually any African or Asian country.[1] The attempt to promote Creole as the official language of the country, for instance, is sometimes cited as the major reason for the loss of power of the Movement Militant Mauricien (MMM) government in 1983 (Bowman, 1991).

While about thirty-three languages are spoken on this small island, Creole, English, and French have captured most prominence, and are regarded as languages of 'egalitarianism,' 'knowledge,' and 'culture' respectively (Philip Baker and Peter Stein, 1991).[2] Arabic, a sacrilegious language, is also used extensively by the Muslim population. Linguistic differences have therefore assumed even more political and social dimensions, adding to the complexity of the Mauritian diversity. The debate over which language is to be used, or included as a medium of expression in the educational system rages on, and as it will be discussed later, it constitutes one of the threats to the political stability of the country.

### Table 6.3
### *Ethnic Composition of Mauritius*

| | |
|---|---|
| Indian and Pakistani Descent | 68.4% |
| European and African Descent | 27.0% |
| Chinese Descent | 2.9% |
| French Descent | 1.9% |

Source: Yang Guilan, Beijing Review, April 1990.

Religious differences have caused many violent political conflicts in Africa. Political problems in Nigeria, Sudan, and Mauritania all have religious undertones. Mauritian society is overwhelmingly religious, with only about 0.2 percent not professing to belong to any religion, but it has managed to avoid the conflicts that multiple religions with sharp differences generate in other societies.

In 1989, Christians, comprising of two overwhelming Catholic groups (the Franco-Mauritians and the Creoles) formed about 30 percent of the entire population. Hindu, however, is the religion of choice for the majority of Mauritians. The significant Muslim population is dominated by the Sunni branch of Islam (Eriksen, 1991). There are also religions of Chinese origins (see table 6.4 for a complete list of religions).

Usually, a highly diverse society as in Mauritius is a recipe for disastrous political conflicts. Contrary to expectation, the country has used its diversity as a strength, and crafted a socio-economic and political system that has been exceptionally productive and also very stable. What then, are the underlying factors to the Mauritian miracle?

## Table 6.4
## *Religious Composition of Mauritius (1983)*

| | |
|---|---|
| Hindus | 52.5% |
| Christians | 30.1% |
| Muslims | 16.6% |
| Chinese Religions | 0.5% |
| Other Religions | 0.1% |
| No Religion | 0.2%* |

Source: Larry Bowman (1991).
*No Religion does not necessarily mean atheism. It could mean unwilling to indicate religious denomination.

*Leadership.* Quality leadership has been responsible for the remarkable transformation of Mauritius, from a country that had severe economic problems to one that has become the envy of all African countries. While it is fair to give credit to elite leaders of all social and political groups, Sir Seewoosagur Ramgoolam's charisma, genius and vision, especially during the early years after independence, laid the foundation for modern Mauritius. He is regarded as the father of the nation (A.R. Mannick, 1989).

Mauritian politics is essentially based on balancing the demands of communities, and Ramgoolam's leadership made an art-form of the politics of coalition. He built a "well-deserved reputation for conciliation, compromise, and an attentiveness to the potential for national unity" (Bowman, 1991, p. 70). He was particularly credited with orchestrating the coalition for national unity when he convinced the influential Sir Gaetan Duval and his party to join the Labor Party to form a government in 1969. This particular coalition, which contributed significantly to Mauritian society comprised of a seemingly impossible political bedmates; Hindus, socialists, wealthy white landowners, Chinese, and working-class Creoles. Such was Ramgoolam's genius for creating consensus for development. His achievements permeates all fabric of Mauritian life, especially in the economic arena.

*The Economy.* Pre-independence Mauritian economy, as has been emphasized earlier, shared the characteristics of many third world countries; geographic isolation from world markets, dense population over a small place, lack of viable markets, mono-crop economy and few natural resources. It also experienced high inflation and acute unemployment problems, with the state over-extending itself in the economic arena (Guilan, 1990).

Within twenty-one years, there has been a radical turnaround. The per-capita GDP of about $3000 has pushed the country into the world middle-level income brackets. By 1988, unemployment had dropped from 11 percent to the negative, inflation had dropped from 30 percent to 2 percent, and the balance of payment had become positive, an almost nonexistent feat in Africa (World Bank, 1989, xv). A mono-crop economy blossomed into a diversified one, with significant contribution from agriculture, manufacturing, and tourism.

There has been a marked improvement in the standard of living. Population growth, which was a major threat at one point, has been purged at a reasonable rate, life expectancy has increased, and so has the doctor-patient ratio. Literacy, which is a keystone to effective political participation is at an African all time high of 95 percent (Guilan, 1990). How was the economy transformed in such a short period of time?

According to Bowman (p. 69), Ramgoolam and most of the political elites responsible for laying the economic foundation believed in Fabian social democracy, fashioning a 'public-private partnership' to build a modern welfare state. An open, export-oriented, market driven strategy was adopted, with specific policies to attract international investments.

The establishment of a duty-free zone (DFZ), and the development of excellent transportation and communication facilities were a few of the sound economic decisions made by the political elites. With 12 international airways flying all over the world, and an advanced sea transportation system, Mauritius' geographic isolation has not posed a problem for international trade (Rolf Alter, 1991). It has also, together with its safe beaches and multiple international languages, increased its volume in the tourism business. Other shrewd policies include the utilization of its triple colonial heritage (French, British, and Dutch) to enjoy membership of both the Francophone-biased Yaounde Convention and the African Caribbean Pacific union (ACP). Through skilled negotiations, Mauritius has managed to gain favorable access to the European markets for its sugar and textile products. But all these achievements would not have been possible, without the effective socio-political choices made to create a stable environment.

*Policies of Inclusion and Consensus.* Most single-party regimes in Africa have argued that because of the extremity of social divisions in their newly created independent states, a multi-party system will breed rancor and divisiveness, justifying their resort to that type of political system (Nyerere, 1968). The Mauritian consociational democracy has proved this contention wrong. Recognizing their plurality, the Mauritian political elites devised a system with constitutional safeguards to accommodate ethnic divisions. Their *spoils system* of parliamentary representation ensures that no section of the population is alienated. A *'national patronage'* system in the form of massive social welfare programs is maintained to cater for the under-privileged in the society.[3]

Free political association has been encouraged, resulting in the formation of many political parties. As expected, political parties have sprung up with strong ethnic identifications. But the freedom of association has also encouraged the incidence of splinter groups within parties, when expectations of all are not met, thereby weakening the influence of ethnic blocs in individual parties. The result has been intra-ethnic rather than inter-ethnic political competition (Eliphas G. Mukonoweshuro, 1991).

With the proliferation of parties, formation of coalitions becomes the only means to form a government, and the ruling elites have turned it into a political resource. Coalitions of all types and styles have been formed within Mauritian politics. The Ramgoolam-Duval government of national unity is just one example. Many government policies have been geared towards benefiting the constituents of coalition parties, thereby encouraging such political associations. One needs to get together with people of other cultural and political background to benefit fully from the government. Material benefits are often the reward of these coalitions, and this fact has shifted direct emphasis from ethnic pride to economic interest.

On the socio-economic front, the government allocates a sizeable portion of its budget to alleviate the hardships of the under-privileged groups. The poor are cushioned from highly priced imported foods through subsidies. A heavy portion of the health care bills are borne by the government. Education at primary, secondary and tertiary levels are free, enabling all to gain at least equal access to the acquisition of skills for the job place (Bowman, 1991).

In addition to equal economic opportunities, respect is also accorded all the various cultures that form the rainbow of Mauritian society. There is freedom of religion and association. For instance, besides the New Year, Independence, and Labor/ May holidays which are celebrated by all, the government allows a celebration of more than twelve other specific holidays (see Table 6.5). The peaceful co-existence of ethnic groups, the respect for different cultures, and the efforts to re-distribute the national cake to benefit all, have all been made possible because of the political system put in place by the political elites of Mauritius.

## Table 6.5
### *Major Holidays in Mauritius*

| | |
|---|---|
| New Year | All |
| Cavadee | Hindu |
| Spring Festival | Chinese |
| Maha Shivaratree | Hindu |
| Independence Day | All |
| Eid-ul-Adha | Muslim |
| Ougadi | Telegu Hindu |
| Easter | Christian |
| Labor/May Day | All |
| Eid-ul-Fitr | Muslim |
| Assumption | Christian |
| Ganesh Chaturti | Marathi Hindu |
| Ganga Snan | Hindu |
| All Saint's Day | Christian |
| Divali | Hindu |
| Christmas | Christian |

Source: Sydney Selvon et. Al.,(1988) cited in L. Bowman (1991).

## Conclusion

Mauritius' achievements in almost all fields are remarkable by all standards. A durable democratic system which is inclusive, effective, and beneficial to all has been established. One of the major factors that has made this possible is the commitment and vision of its leadership. Sir Ramgoolam laid the foundation for independent Mauritius, and subsequent leaders including the current Prime Minister, Sir Aneerood

Jugnauth have continued to provide the quality leadership that has been the hallmark of the country.

Mauritius recognized the heterogeneity of its society and crafted a political system that is relevant to its history, blending aspects of British parliamentary system and Mauritian communal authority structure. The result has been a successful utilization of the concept of coalitions to cater for the demands of the various sections of the society.

The choices made by the elite leadership gained the approval of the international business community, resulting in an appreciable in-flow of investments. The country has also utilized its triple colonial heritage to align itself solidly with major European industrial powers and also gained access to their markets, including the North American markets. Will Mauritius continue to enjoy the same international financial support? Does the country has a foundation strong enough to sustain any major future disruptions? Given the resurgence of ethnic identification in politics worldwide, can the consociational arrangement of the democratic system withstand any further structural challenge?

Much will depend on the choices to be made by the ruling elites. Ironically, one of the strengths of the political system is the relatively balanced pull from all the many communities. The absence of an indigenous population has helped Mauritius to reducethe tension normally created by the feeling of usurpation habored by groups in many such countries. The fact that all Mauritians have outside roots increases the respect they have for one another. It also enhances the desire to make the politics of consensus more attractive.

Mauritius has its share of problems just like any country (A.R. Mannick, 1989). Currently, the adoption of the Creole language for instruction in all schools is brewing a political storm. It has the potential of causing political rifts based along ethnic lines. The elites have overcome similar problems in the past, and should be able to keep this rainbow nation together.

# Notes to Chapter Eight

1.    Cited in Bowman, 1991.

2.    *Ibid.*

3.    See Eliphas G. Mukonoweshuro (1991) for an elaboration on the Spoil System and the National Patronage system.

# Questions to Chapter Eight

1. Why is the ethnic composition important for democracy in Mauritius?

2. What factors account for the remarkable economic as well as political success of Mauritius?

## CHAPTER NINE

# THE SEARCH FOR AN AFRICAN DEMOCRACY MODEL

## Introduction

In the social sciences, there has not been an agreed upon definition of consolidated democracy (see Adam Przeworski et al. 1996). This study operationalizes an African consolidated democracy as one that has stuck to its democratic constitution, and has enjoyed at least more than three consecutive rounds of competitive elections, with the result being accepted by the opposition and the international community. As simple as this definition may be, it offers a good platform to determine which transitions have come to stay and which ones were cosmetic. It provides a good criteria for comparative analysis. Consolidation in real terms, however, will mean having a permanent system of democratic governance.

Sustaining the recent democratic gains has become the major occupation of advocates for democracy, both in Africa and the outside world. Many doubts are being raised, and justifiably so (given the past experience of democracy in Africa), about the ability and capacity of the political systems which have undergone democratic transitions recently, to keep to their constitutions in subsequent changes of government (Adam Przeworski and Fernando Limongi, 1995).

Numerous obstacles stand in the way of such progress, given the frailties of the African socio-political environment. Such fears have provided grounds for a contention that the recent trend is just a fleeting occurrence. Some of these problems have been discussed in earlier chapters. A brief examination of the rest of them will lay the foundation for a critical examination of Africa's chances for consolidated democracy.

## Obstacles

The failure of previous transitions to democracy has led many scholars to conclude that Africa lacks the necessary linchpins for sustainable democracy (Zaffiro, 1989). The argument is that since the current efforts at democratization do not display much of the necessary credentials of an enduring democracy, it would be illusory to expect sustainable democracy to result from it (John B. Londregan and Keith T. Poole, 1990).

Doubts about the durability of the current democratic exercise have been based on the lack of certain conditions in Africa; conditions such as the existence of a market-oriented economy, higher levels of economic well-being, education, and urbanization (John F. Helliwell, 1993). The heterogeneity of ethnic groups in African states and a dogged clinging to old traditions are also some of the hindrances to democratic consolidation. Do these conditions necessarily act as constraints to democratic sustenance in Africa? Are they the only conditions for consolidation?

A market-oriented economy decentralizes political power; private entrepreneurs get to control a significant part of the economy, and economic power often times translates into political power. As power becomes dispersed in a liberalized economy, more people develop an interest in the rules of the game to keep it fair and efficient. Free market system demands the cultivation of active participation and competition, the same elements required for a successful functioning of a democratic political system. A successful operation of a free market, therefore lays the infrastructure for a democratic culture which facilitate democratic consolidation.

Few African countries can boast of a market-oriented economy. The state in Africa plays a major role in the economy. African governments, in addition to setting the conditions under which individuals and corporations must operate, have themselves become the main employers. African economies suffer from the problems of over-extended states. Public expenditure per Gross Domestic Product in Africa is higher than in the industrialized as well as other developing economies.

Zambia for instance, has a 25 percent ratio of public consumption to GDP, compared to a weighted mean of 17 percent for industrial market-oriented economies with rather large welfare programs (Chazan et al., 1992, p. 269).

The desire to increase political leverage and the shortage of private entrepreneurial skills have pushed the African state to take on too many tasks. From the managing of agricultural produce (a task that can easily and profitably be performed by the private sector), to the heavy involvement in education and the health sector, governments have stifled individual initiatives not only in the economic sector but in the social and political realms as well. Needless to say, the over-extended state creates in its wake inefficiencies, corruption, and strong patron-client relationship. The civic space needed for creativity and effective private check on state abuses is therefore denied.

The citizen, having become increasingly dependent on the government, loses the power to confront it in cases of abuse and misuse of power. The consequent patron-client relationship allows the government to get away with undemocratic practices such as human rights abuses and encourages it to become even more repressive when its rule is challenged. In effect, in non-market-oriented societies, the state extends itself to the point where there is no space for any effective political activity independent of the government. Democracy suffers because governments are not held accountable.

Another often debated issue closely related to the role of the market in democracies is the relationship between economic well-being of a country and its political system (see for example, Przeworski and Limongi, 1995; Robert J. Barro, 1994). Economic development or development as a whole, as discussed already and illustrated in the correlation scatter plot, generally scores higher in democracies than in authoritarian societies.

An industrialized society is an affluent society. Abbas Pourgerami (1991, p. 179) has argued that wealth "moderates the tension of political conflict and offers greater economic resources for accommodation and compromise." He reiterates the argument of wealth creating a middle class, which becomes the

most influential in taking political, social, and economic decisions in a country. The assumption is that it is in the interest
of the members of this middle class to ensure a political system
which is democratic, because a freer and fairer society increases the potential for upward mobility. An absence or a
smaller middle class in any society therefore is a setback to
democratic consolidation.

A combination of factors has deprived Africa of a dominant middle class, and the advantages it brings to the politics
of a society. Africa was under colonial rule for a period of time,
and colonial interests were not compatible with the creation of
a large middle class because of the fear of the potential of this
class providing a viable challenge to colonial privileges. The denial for opportunities that encourage the formation of this
class has robbed the politics of post-colonial Africa.

In spite of the independence, the structure of African
economies has not changed significantly from what it used to
be in the colonial era. The personnel running the new countries changed hands but the policies remained the same, irrespective of the ideological persuasion of the leaders. The trading ties that existed between Britain and its former colonies or
France and its newly independent states have remained almost
intact. The result is that, just as in the colonial times, only few
elites control the political and economic destinies of these
countries. When the military blazed its way into politics to
break the meritocracy that was becoming the system of government, a system of new but small ruling elites was added to
those who were already in control.

Elite control of societies is not unique to Africa. The
unique character of the African situation is that not only is the
elite class unproductive economically, it also stifles initiatives
that will produce another class (the middle class) which is believed to generate economic growth. The chances for the creation of a middle class grew even slimmer with the introduction
of the military into politics.

In discussing the problems of development in Africa, it
would be unfair to ignore the undemocratic nature of the international economic system and its adverse impact on African

economic policies. The international economic system is based on self interest, and newly independent states with little political and economic clout operate within it from a very disadvantaged position. With their economic roles perked at being suppliers of raw materials, African states have had no real control over the pricing of their produce in a market where the prices of manufactured goods (mostly from outside the continent) as well as capital, have continued to rise, creating unfavorable terms of trade. The result is that African economies have become shackled under severe debts and unequal trading relationships, strangling any economic growth that sound policies may have the chance to generate.

Mention should also be made of the adverse effects that cold war politics have on African economies and political systems. Strategic interests of major world powers married selfish intentions of African leaders to create a system where "friendly autocrats" were actively supported and maintained by powerful external democracies.

But whatever the reasons are, it is an undeniable fact that African societies are at the bottom of the world in terms of economic affluence. Their economies are not growing at an appreciable rate that may raise their standards of living any time soon to the levels of the industrial democracies. The absence of a sizeable middle class combines with the other factors to hamper the growth of a democratic system. But should not the educated elites be conscious of these facts and devise strategies of overcoming them? What role has education played in the consolidation of democracy in Africa?

Adopting the definition of Morrison et al. (1989 p. 51), education is generally seen as a "consciously pursued or programmatic phase of acculturation that is observed in all societies." Education is sometimes viewed narrowly as a conservative force insuring the perpetuation of existing traditions. Education in Africa however, has been a key instrument of transition. While agreeing with Clignet and Foster (1966) about the elite formation role of education in Africa, their conclusion on its impact in Africa is debatable.

Clignet and Foster argue that education has accelerated individual social mobility, but the opportunities it created were for only certain privileged members of society. They contend that the "elite" effect of education has therefore tended to intensify "ethnic identification and inequalities based on such perceived identity."[1] As argued in an earlier chapter, contrary to dominant assumptions, elites, when they do share a common interest in the progress of their country, stand a better chance of executing a more durable democratic transition with a better chance of consolidation. Creation of elites therefore may not necessarily be detrimental to democracy in Africa (refer to the role of elites in a top-down transition). It can also be argued that creating elites from different ethnic groups, as the educational systems of some African countries do, is in itself a unifying factor because of its cross-cutting effects. This is a plus for democratic consolidation because it helps in levelling the field among various ethnic groups. In Ghana for instance, education from primary up to the tertiary level is funded by the government, and this brings together people from all ethnic, religious, and class groups. The only criteria for admission is academic merit, and since the government bears all the financial responsibilities, secondary schools and university campuses become centers of melting pots of ethnic, religious and class groups.

Education also plays an important role in transforming social values. It stimulates participation in modern institutions. David Lerner (1958), S. N. Eisenstadt (1972), and more directly Gabriel Almond and Sydney Verba (1963) have all confirmed the potency of education as a value-inculcating agent, and more importantly as a stimulant of political participation. Almond and Verba actually posited a direct positive relationship between education and political participation in their 1963 study.

Africa came late to the formal type of education, given its historical relationship with the West. However, the last thirty years have seen a phenomenal growth of formal education in the continent.[2] In spite of its restricted universal access and the danger of creating a deeper rift between the masses and the elite, education if properly dispensed, has the potential of developing a sense of national identification. It transcends ethnic and other divisive loyalties. It may also assist in the internalization of certain positive attitudes, which may in the long run auger well for democratic consolidation.

Urbanization has been cited as one of the factors that initially hinders democratic development (Pourgerami, 1991).[3] Urbanization and industrialization it is argued, sharpen already existing social cleavages such as ethnic, religious, and class divisions. In an environment of uncertainty and anonymity (which urban dwellers constantly find themselves), it may be argued that people tend to cling to the comfort of ethnic, religious and other social groups that they are mostly familiar with. In an attempt to carve a position for themselves, urban dwellers get caught up in a competitive environment which create social and political tensions. Such tensions, if not properly managed can be disastrous to democracy.

This argument has merits but only in the short run. In the long run, however, urbanization may contribute to democratic consolidation. Urbanization re-arranges the traditional social matrix, bringing people of different backgrounds together, in the process modifying their traditional world-view. Such a process may also create new social alliances, demanding a more complex but civic way of relating to each other to solve the more complicated problems of urban life.

In addition, urban centers, being the loci for information sharing about one's country and its relationship with the outside world, may provide the building blocs for a process of national identification. This can easily be used to rally support for national institutions which may advance democratic principles.

Africa is probably the least urbanized continent, with the majority of its people living in small towns and villages, but it is also the fastest urbanizing of all the continents. According to Morrison et al. (p. 60), Africa had a 30% growth in urbanization between 1950 and 1960, as compared to the world's 19%, and North America's 14%. This is a positive trend. Given the discussed negative relationship between urbanization and social cohesion initially, it may seem that the current growth rate of urbanization in Africa will hamper the development of democracy.

Africa's urban growth, however, is different from the West in a number of ways. In the West, urbanization normally occurs with industrialization. In Africa, not much industrialization has occurred, deepening the dependency of urban dwellers on the government thereby worsening the level of competition for scarce resources. This exacerbates even further the social and political tensions normally associated with urban growth.

Urbanization occurring without industrialization may create negative consequences for democratic development, and in this sense, urbanization in Africa may seem to pose even a greater danger to democratic consolidation than had already been expected in the West. On the other hand, the African urban dweller does not typically break ties with the extended family in the rural area. Most Africans in the urban centers, being the first migrant dwellers maintain a very close relationship with the rest of the family in the towns or villages they migrate from. They are regular visitors to their former towns and villages and may therefore not feel the extreme rootlessness a typical urban migrant in the West may feel.

The extended family system of most African societies, where family is defined in broader terms than in the West, also contributes to strengthening the relationship between the urban and rural centers. Such a tradition weakens the normally deep sense of alienation urban dwellers face. Tradition therefore mitigates the normally hostile attitudes people of different social background foster for each other in urban settings.

Urban centers in Africa, because of their stronger ties with the rural areas, influence national development more than it is normally assumed. These ties also facilitate information exchange between the urban dweller and the rural folks, making government activities more understandable to those far away from the center of power. In view of this fact, the role of urbanization in democratic consolidation is more crucial in Africa than in the West. In the short run, it may seem a threat to democracy but ultimately, urbanization helps in developing a democratic culture. One ought to be cautious, however, in evaluating the weight of urbanization in the democratic consolidation equation, since it has to combine with other equally critical variables to be effective. What variables then, are the most critical in sustaining democracy in Africa?

## Consolidating Conditions

It must be emphasized from the outset that there is no one set of sufficient conditions for democratic consolidation applicable to all societies. Different societies have had different historical experiences. Some societies are more vulnerable to certain historical factors such as ethnic rivalries or religious divisions than others. Diversity in certain countries may be a plus while in others, it may be a disaster for national cohesion. A discussion of conditions necessarily for consolidation is therefore, one essentially based on generalizations, using individual successes as a guide. Individual countries may have to examine and apply a combination of conditions in the set which are most relevant to their specific circumstances.

Based on the experiences of consolidated democracies such as Botswana and Mauritius, it may be argued that variables such as good leadership (both at personal and group levels), appropriate political structures (in the form of institutions), appreciable levels of economic development (in the long run), reasonable level of civility, and genuine external support may combine to create a democratic culture which will consolidate democracy in Africa.

Democratic culture in this context defines attitudes, beliefs, and behavior that is accepting of diversity, competition, and moderation of views in the majority of the population. It is the environment where the political system has been tried and been accepted by key groups in the society as being relatively fair and efficient. It is the stage where institutions of society are seen as legitimate by the majority of the people. A brief examination of these variables in an African context will illuminate this proposition.

*Development.* The correlation between development and consolidated democracies has already been established in an earlier chapter. It is worth reiterating, however, that while socio-economic decline especially, may actually precipitate a transition to democracy, a society will need a higher level of socio-economic development in the long run, to be able to consolidate its democratic gains. The strong correlation of democracy and development in Botswana and Mauritius is a confirmation of this contention. Continued periods of economic decline or stagnation may erode the legitimacy of the new democratic regime, providing grounds for either an overthrow of the democratic government by the military, or a backslide to authoritarianism to stop the imminent protests that are bound to come from the people. Gambia, which had a long standing democracy in spite of declining levels of development came to an end abruptly with the military take-over recently. Economics cannot be left out in the consolidation equation for long.

*Civic Space.* The necessity of a civil society to democratic consolidation has also been discussed extensively in social science literature (see for example, Vaclav Havel, Vaclav Klaus and Petr Pithart, 1996; Wilmot James and Daria Caliguire, 1996). Consolidation depends partially on the availability of civic space to check the abuses of the self-serving state. There should be a forum for the discussion of government activities in a civil manner. One of the major strengths of Botswana's democracy is the Kgotla and the Freedom Square systems which allow regular examination of the governments performance. Such an exercise helps in legitimizing the system because the citizens see themselves as part of the system. It also teaches the importance of disagreeing in a civil manner. A civil society regulates the tensions in the society and inculcates in the people attitudes and behavioral patterns that are supportive of democratic institutions. It also encourages adherence to the rule of law, one of the pillars of democracy.

*Leadership.* Leadership plays an important role in politics, even more so in Africa. The leadership factor comes in at two levels; the qualities of the individual at the helm of national affairs and those of the leaders representing significant groups in the country (be it in the political, social, or economic realm). Dunkwart Rustow (1970) has argued to the contrary that, the consolidation of democracy depends on factors other than the qualities and strategies of principal actors. A critical study of Africa's political history, however, contradicts this viewpoint.

From pre-colonial times to the period of liberation of the continent from colonialism (this period characterized by some as the first wave of democratization), up to the present day, Africa's political history is replete with personalities being the main source of political change. From the Shaka de Zulus of the Nguni people who single-handedly revolutionalized the political system of his region through to Kwame Nkrumah of modern day Ghana whose personal leadership style left significant imprints on the political systems of his country and Africa as a whole, personal leadership has played a monumental role in African politics. The ideological inclination and personal commitment of the leader is crucial to the success of any chosen political path. It may be argued that the main resource of Mauritius' successes is the quality of its leadership, given the fact that it has relatively no natural resources. Currently though, it appears that those countries that have been successful in democratic systems have done it with group leadership. Elites or group leaders have in both Botswana and Mauritius, collectively consented to a direction of their political systems and manage to convince the rest of the people to the viability of the chosen direction.

This viewpoint is compatible with the earlier discussed top-down theory where elite consensus becomes very crucial to the success of the democratic transition. Botswana's Seretse Khama and Mauritius Seewoosagur Ramgoolam may not be as famous as the Nkrumahs and the Nyereres but they have led their countries to achieve democracy and economic development mostly through the generation of consensus among the elites of various groups in their societies.

In Botswana, even though the foundation of the current political system was laid by the late Sir Seretse Khama, it was mostly the leaders of the eight main ethnic groups that have maintained and supported the democratic system. Khama died in 1980 but the democratic culture has grown stronger because of the commitment of the elites.

Mauritius, being one of the countries with many social cleavages, has undergone many constitutional changes in its brief political history after independence. It has moved from a Constitutional Monarchy to a Republic, but all within the framework of a multi-party parliamentary system. This has been possible due to the consensus and commitment of leaders of racial, ethnic, religious and class groupings. The people with good leadership have developed a stake in the politics of the country, making the system work effectively.

Leadership has therefore come in two forms in Africa; either a towering individual who is committed and has the singular vision, courage and capacity to move the country in a particular direction, or the leaders of various groups consenting to move their country in the desired political direction.

*Political Institutions.* The choice of the right political system for Africa has been one of the often debated issues.[4] The merits and demerits of the parliamentary system which most former British colonies in Africa inherited, and the presidential and quasi-presidential systems adopted by some African countries have been the topic of discussion in many other studies (see for instance, Alfred Stepan and Cindy Skach, 1993; Arend Lijphart, 1992; Juan J. Linz, 1990).

At independence, the departing colonial authorities ensured that its former colonies including Ghana, Kenya, Gambia and Nigeria, adopted the much cherished parliamentary System of Britain. The parliamentary system was once described as the "jewel" of British colonization.[5] Sooner than later, either individual leaders or the elites of the newly independent countries became disenchanted with the system and tampered with it, removing most of the in-built checks on the executive. With time, Prime Minister Nkrumah of Ghana for instance, became President Nkrumah with excessive executive powers, having tampered with the constitution to that effect.

The adoption or conversion to presidential systems went a bit further than it pertains in the West. In successful bids to remove or cripple opposition, presidential positions became personalized, and the line between the office and the person occupying the office became blurry. Such a move made it possible for instance, for Arap Moi to be 'anointed' as the official successor to the ageing President Jomo Kenyatta without any serious competitive elections. This trend was followed in different forms and to different degrees in many other countries including Tanzania where Ali Hassan Mwinyi replaced Julius Nyerere.

The next logical sequence was the introduction of the one-party system where opposition was effectively eliminated from the political scene. Justification was provided by African scholars citing the unique situation of African politics and the need for unity under one national leadership. The potential explosiveness of the ethnic factor in newly independent African states became an excuse for the institution of single-party systems. Competitive multi-party system was seen as a recipe for rancor, acrimony and divisiveness.[6] President Robert Mugabe for instance, has adamantly stuck to this position, even in recent times when such arguments have become untenable and empirically indefensible. These attitudes paved the way for, and justified the single party systems that became the favorite ploy of African leaders who sought to perpetuate themselves in power. Institutions were twisted to generate unsurpassed powers for the executive, virtually erasing the powers of the other branches of government that ensure a check on misuse and abuse of executive power.

Many factors account for the failure of both the presidential and parliamentary systems in Africa. Many African leaders for instance, transplanted Western models into African societies without any adjustment, ignoring the fact that their political histories are different from that of the West. The euphoria of independence from colonial rule blinded many of them to commit such mistakes. This error in judgement gives ammunition to traditionalists who call for a return to Africa's past to look for political solutions to modern problems. But such a move has its limitations as well.

Africa's post-colonial ethnic problems make it imperative that the political system adopted is sensitized to the needs of all groups. As argued earlier, the composition of ethnic groups in a country by itself may not generate serious conflicts. It is the denial of access to the political process of some groups in post-colonial Africa that is the main source of ethnic conflict. Any viable system must therefore adopt either a constitutional mechanism or an electoral system that seeks to include all groups in the political process. A form of proportional representation that will make it possible for minority ethnic groups to be represented meaningfully will help reduce the feeling of alienation by the smaller groups.

The world is modernizing and things may never go back to the "good old days." The cry for Africa to go back totally to a "glorious" traditional past is therefore as unfeasible as the attempts to impose a totally alien system on a society with a different historical experience.

Africa before colonialism had democratic as well as authoritarian political systems. There were wide variations in political authority and systems. The Tutsi of Rwanda and Burundi and the Amhara of Ethiopia for instance, had highly centralized political systems which were not quite democratic. The Tiv of Nigeria were totally different, in the sense that they had a decentralized and a relatively more democratic political system. In between these two extremes, the Akan of modern day Ghana and the Yoruba of Nigeria combined "principles of chieftaincy with principles of representative democracy, notably elected councils" (Morrison et al, pp. 8–9).

A call to abandon totally Western political institutions for pre-colonial African authority structures can therefore be misleading and confusing because of the wide variations in traditional authority structures. It is not feasible mainly because many groups with different political structures have been put together to form the new African nation states. A choice of traditional institutions should be done carefully to avoid the risk of imposing one tradition over other groups who may not share that tradition, given the fact that modern African states are comprised of many groups who historically did not live together. Given the interdependent relationship in a world gone global and modern, one ought to be careful not to throw away the good aspects of modernity which are relevant for the sake of traditions which may not be relevant today.

There is also the need to distinguish between what is modern and what is Western (Ali A. Mazrui, 1990). There is a tendency to equate the two. Africa can modernize in relevant areas without necessarily westernizing culturally. Usually, it is the wholesale adoption of Western culture, aspects of which can clash with traditional mores, that fuel nationalistic feeling among traditionalists and fundamentalists.

A balance should be drawn between tradition and modernity. Traditions, contrary to some modernization theories, do not necessarily impede development. Some traditions may actually enhance the drive towards modernization if they are skillfully modified. There is the need to identify certain traditional institutions and practices which can be modernized and made relevant to contemporary societies. Once again, the Kgotla system in Botswana serves as an example of a traditional institution that has been adopted to serve the needs of a modern society. Ghana's current constitution also recognizes the importance of the institution of Chieftaincy, and it has incorporated it into its modern political set up. Among its responsibilities, the legally empowered National House of Chiefs (section 272, c, p. 165) has been charged to do, among other things to:

> undertake an evaluation of traditional customsand
> usages with a view to eliminating those customs and
> usages that are outmoded and socially harmful.

Such an exercise, after ridding the society of retrogressive traditions can bring the surviving ones to re-inforce the newly established institutions and its mores. In Britain for instance, the political system includes some old traditions such as the Monarchy and the House of Lords. Some of Japan's neo-feudal traditions have been incorporated into its modern philosophy of production with amazing results. The notion of a zero-sum relationship between modernity and tradition should be eschewed.

The failure of the Western political models in immediate post-colonial Africa could also be attributed partly to inadequate preparation of political elites who took over after independence (Basil Davidson, 1993). The colonial political structure was essentially a hierarchical and undemocratic one. The African elites who replaced the colonial administrators combined inexperience with greed to take over the "ex-colonial paradise." Parliamentary and presidential systems were accepted for lack of any worked out alternative, and in due course, some selfish elites manipulated it to make it more pliable to their needs. It is therefore wrong to reject totally foreign models just because they are foreign. There is the need to adopt aspects, which can be relevant to the African situation as has been done in Botswana. What kind of political system then, is appropriate for post-independent Africa?

Societies are products of their histories. Different societies have taken different routes in arriving at where they are now. In as much as Africa shares many commonalities, there are historical events unique to each country. Europe may have in general terms, democratic political systems, but different historical experiences have informed and shaped each individual political system; hence the differences in for example, the British, the French and the Swedish democracies.

Botswana's democratic system may be characterized as paternalistic by outsiders, but its nature is deeply influenced by its political history.[7] The Kgotla system which has its roots in history has been incorporated into the new British parliamentary system and it has worked successfully. It is performing the functions expected of it in a fair, free, and accountable manner. Mauritius came under both French and British rule. Its political system reflects the Franco-British political traditions as well as the other cultural experiences of its Asian and African population.

Each African country needs to examine critically its history and design a political system that draws from its past experiences, and yet addresses the realities of today. Such a model will not have legitimacy problems because it will not ignore past institutions, which are still strong and adhered to by the majority of the people at the community level. The impact of colonialism, to some extent, may be superficial because loyalties to pre-colonial traditions that are still fairly strong. Given the recent past political experience in Africa and elsewhere, constitution engineers need to bare in mind that accountability, responsiveness, and participation by the people (pillars of democracy) are crucial ingredients in drawing up a constitution that will gain the approval of the majority of the people. Unwarranted restrictions on political and civil liberties may deprive the system of the legitimacy that is needed for consolidation.

A discussion of institutions and political conflict in Africa will not be complete without the mention of the military. Military intervention has become one of the major means of government change in Africa (see S. E. Quainoo, 1994, a paper presented at the New York African Studies Conference, New Paltz). The notion that the military is professionally barred from politics is alien to Africa. Traditionally, all able-bodied citizens have been involved in defending the nation and contributing to the political process as well. With the current level of involvement of the military in politics all over the continent, it will be unfeasible to totally deny them any form of direct political activity. Constitutions should therefore allow the military some form of participation. The nature and degree of political involvement will depend on the history of the military in a specific country.

*External Support.* External support for countries that have undergone democratic transitions is essential for the nature and eventual consolidation of the democratic gains made. External support can come from two sources, the international community at large and from within Africa. Established democracies within Africa should come to the aid of new democracies in the form of moral, economic, and political support. Africa cannot boast of many consolidated democracies with strong economic backgrounds to offer material assistance but the moral and psychological effect of having a successful democracy within the sub-region is important.

The role of industrial democracies in the West is also crucial. A fairer form of political conditionality attached to economic aid is necessary to discourage dictators. Leaders moving in the right direction should be assisted, along the lines offered to Aristide of Haiti. This is not an advocation for external intervention, neither is it a call for importation of western models. This has been the mistake of the past. Larry Diamond (1992, p. 27) while urging the United States to promote democracy abroad cautioned against this tendency of the past:

> Promoting democracy does not mean exporting it. Except in rare instances, democracy does not work when foreign models are imposed, and many features of American democracy are ill-suited to poor, unstable and divided societies.

Promotion should come in the form of rewarding African countries that are instituting democratic reforms with economic and diplomatic support. Significant economic aid for instance, will cushion the short term pains of democratic societies restructuring their economic systems to respond to the initial bumps in the market-oriented system. Ghana has enjoyed a relatively high level of support from the international financial community and this has helped in avoiding to a great extent, the dangers of unfulfilled expectations in the short run.

Foreign assistance may also be directed at strengthening nongovernmental democratic institutions that are set up in the individual African countries. A strong show of approval by the international community, backed by rewards to democracies and a denial of moral and material support to authoritarian leaders will contribute to democratic consolidation in Africa.

## Prospects

It may be argued that a combination of astute and committed leadership, a market-oriented economy, a civic society, and external support may combine to create a democratic culture, which will lead to a consolidated democracy (see figure 7.1). The right combination will depend on the historical experience of the individual country, bearing in mind its areas of vulnerability and strength. There is the need to make use of the traditions in specific countries that support democratic principles, and reform those that act as barriers. While emphasizing that no one recipe exists for democratic consolidation, the above discussed variables can be instrumental in the consolidation of democracies in Africa.

## Figure 7.1
## AN AFRICAN DEMOCRATIC MODEL

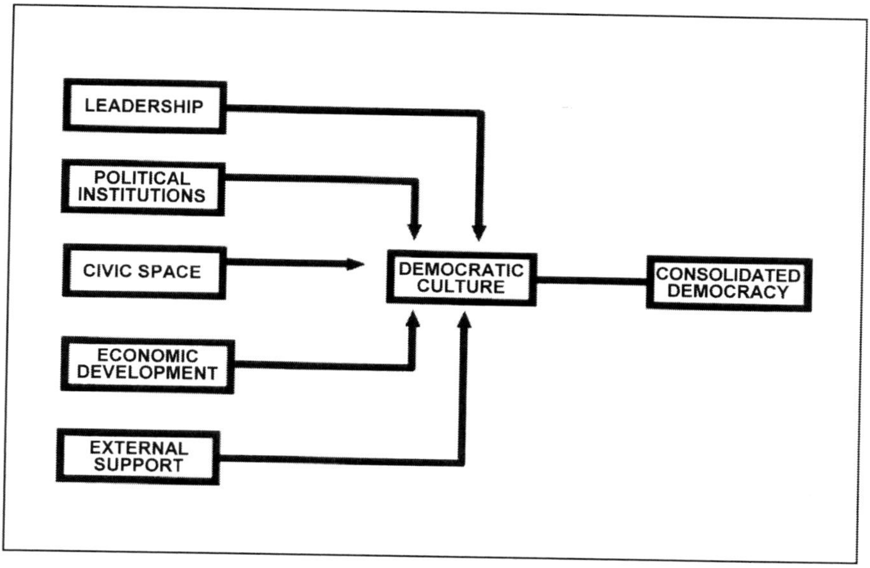

Africa may not possess the required socio-economic conditions as argued by Lipset for democratic consolidation, but those requirements are not sufficient conditions for democratic consolidation in Africa. The African experience shows that there are many different paths to democratic consolidation. The current crop of democracies mushrooming in Africa may not all survive the turn of the century, but those that allow their history to inform the crafting of their new political systems, tailoring it to the unique demands of their societies, may make the democratic journey successfully.

## Notes to Chapter Nine

1.    This quote is cited in Morrison et al, (1989), p. 51.

2.    *Ibid.*

3.    For specifics, see Pourgerami, 1991, p. 179.

4.    See for example, Munslow, 1983, and Tordoff, 1993.

5.    See Ali Mazrui's recorded series on Africa. It appears under the 'New Conflicts' volume.

6.    Other leaders who have used this argument include Jerry Rawlings of Ghana, until he became 'converted' to multiparty system of government.

7.    See Larry Diamond, ed. (1988).

# Questions to Chapter Nine

1.  What are the main obstacles to consolidated democracy in Africa?

2.  What are the factors that favor democratic consolidation in Africa?

# REFERENCES

*Africa Confidential.* vol. 33. No. 1, 10 January 1992, p. 1.

Ake, Claude. "The Unique Case of African Democracy." *International Affairs*, 69, (April 1993), pp. 239–44.

————. "As Africa Democratises." *Africa Forum*, vol. 1, No. 2, 1991.

————. *Revolutionary Pressures in Africa.* London: Zed Press, 1978.

————. *Social Science as Imperialism: A theory of Political Development.* Ibadan University Press, 1979.

————. *The New World Order: A View from the South.* Lagos: Malthouse Press, 1992.

Almond, G., and Verba, S. *The Civic Culture.* Boston: Little Brown, 1963.

Apter, D. E. *Political Change, Collected Essays.* London, F. Cass, 1973.

Aran, L., Einsenstadt, S.N., and Adler, C. "The Effectiveness of Educational Systems in the Process of Modernization." *Comparative Education Review* 16, Feb. 1972.

Bachrach, Peter. *The Theory of Democratic Elitism; A critique.* Boston, Little, Brown, 1967.

————. *Ghana in Transition.* New York, Atheneum, 1963.

Banks, A. S., Day A. J., and Muller, T. C. ed., *Political Handbook of the World 1995–1996.* CSA Publications, Binghamton University, Binghamton, N.Y., 1995.

Banks, A. S. *A Cross-Polity Survey.* Cambridge, M.I.T. Press, 1963.

————. *Cross-National Time Series, 1815–1973,* Ann Arbor, Michigan, ICPSR, 1976.

Benedict, B. *Mauritius; The Problems of a Plural Society.* London: Pall Mall Press, 1965.

Berg-Schlosser, D. *Tradition and Change in Kenya: A comparative analysis of seven major ethnic groups.* Paderborn: F. Schoning, c.1984.

————. *Political Stability and Development: A Comparative Analysis of Kenya, Tanzania, and Uganda.* Boulder: L. Rienner Publishers, 1990.

Bjornlund, E. Bratton M., and Gibson, C. "Observing Multiparty Elections in Africa: Lessons from Zambia." *African Affairs.* Vol. 91 (July 1992), pp. 405–31.

Bollen, Kenneth. "Liberal Democracy: Validity and Method Factors in Cross-National Measures, American." *Journal of Political Science,* vol. 37 (Nov. 1993), pp. 1207–30.

Bowman, L. W., Mauritius. "Democracy and Development in the Indian Ocean." *Westview Press,* 1991.

Bratton, M., and Liatto-Katundu, B. *A Focus Group Assessment of Political Attitudes in Zambia.* African Affairs (1994), 93, 535–563.

Budge, Ian, and Hofferbert Richard I. "The Party Mandate and the Westminster Model: Election Programmes and Government Spending in Britain." *British Journal of Political Science.* Vol. 22 (April 1992), pp. 151–82.

Burnell, Peter. "Zambia At The Crossroads." *World Affairs.* Vol. 157, (Summer 1994), pp. 19–28.

Busia, K. *Purposeful Education for Africa* (The Hague: Mouton, 1964.

Caron, B. et al., ed., *Democratic Transition in Africa.* CREDU, Nigeria, 1992.

Chabal, P. "Democracy in Africa." *International Affairs* 70, 1, 1994.

Chazan N. et al., *Politics and Society in Contemporary Africa.* Lynne Rienner Publishers, Inc., 1992.

Clignet R. and Foster, P. *The Fortunate Few.* Northwestern University Press, 1966.

Cohen R. and Goulbourne, H. ed., *Democracy and Socialism in Africa.* Boulder: Westview Press, 1991.

Colclough, C. *The Political Economy of Botswana: A study of Growth and Distribution.* Oxford University Press, 1980.

Crook, R. C. "Legitimacy, Authority and the Transfer of Power in Ghana." *Political Studies* (1987), XXXV, pp. 553–72.

Curry Jr., R. L. "Adaptation of Botswana's Development Strategy to Meet Its Peoples' Needs for Land, Jobs." *American Journal of Economics and Sociology,* vol. 45, No. 3 (July 1986).

Dahl, Robert Alan. *Polyarchy; Participation and Opposition,* New Haven. Yale University Press, 1971.

———. *Democracy, Liberty, and Equality.* New York, 1986.

———. *Modern Political Analysis.* N.J., Prentice-Hall 1970.

————.*Democracy and its Critics*. New Haven: Yale University Press, 1989.

Davidson, B. *African Civilization Revisited*. Africa World Press, Trenton, New Jersey, 1993.

Decalo, S. "The Process, Prospects and Constraints of Democratization in Africa." *African Affairs* 91, 1992, pp. 7–35.

Dodd, C.H. *Democracy and Development in Turkey*. N. Humberside: Eothen Press, 1979.

Diamond, L. "Rethinking Civil Society." *Journal of Democracy*, July 1994.

————. "Promoting Democracy." *Foreign Affairs*, v. 87, summer 1992, pp. 25–46.

————. "Economic Development and Democracy Reconsidered." *American Behavioral Scientist*, 33 4/5, pp. 450–99.

Diamond, L., Lipset, S. M., and Linz, J. "Building and Sustaining Democratic Government in Developing Countries: Some Tentative Findings." *Comparative Political Studies*, vol. 150, No. 1, Summer 1987.

Gastil, Raymond D. *Comparative Survey of Freedom. 1972–1976*. Ann Arbor, Michigan: ICPSR ed. 1977.

Good K. "Debt and the One-Party State in Zambia." *The Journal of Modern African Studies* 27, 2 (1989), pp. 297–313.

————. "Interpreting the Exceptionality of Botswana." *Journal of Modern African Studies* 30 (1): 69–95, 1992.

Guilan, Yang. "Mauritius in Rapid Economic Development." *Beijing Review*, vol. 33 (April 2nd, 1990), pp. 16–17.

Gyimah-Boadi, E. *Africa Today*. 4th Quarter, 1991, pp. 5–15.

Ham, Melinda. "End of the Honeymoon." *Africa Report*, vol. 37, (May/June 1992), pp. 58–60.

————. "History Repeats Itself." *Africa Report*, vol. 38 (May/June 1993), pp. 13–16.

Hagopian, F. "Democracy by Undemocratic Means? Elites, Political Pacts, and Regime Transition in Brazil." *Comparative Political Studies* 23, 147–70.

Harbeson, J. W., Rothchild, D., and Chazan, N. *Civil Society and the State in Africa*. Lynne Rienner Publishers, Boulder, 1994.

Hanna, W.J., and Hanna J.L. *Urban Dynamics in Black Africa: An Interdisciplinary Approach*, New York: Aldine, 1981.

Havel V., Klaus, V., and Pithart P. "Rival Visions." *Journal of Democracy*, vol. 7, No. 1, January 1996, pp. 12–23.

Healey, J. *Democracy, Governance and Economic Policy: Sub-Saharan Africa in Comparative Perspective*. London: Overseas Development Agency, 1992.

Helliwell, J. F. "Structural Adjustment and The Environment" (book review). *Environmental Science and Technology*, vol. 27 (May 1993), p. 817.

Herbst, J. I. *The Politics of Reform in Ghana, 1982–1991*. Berkeley: University of California Press, 1993.

Hertz, J. ed., *From Dictatorship to Democracy: Coping with the Legacies of Authoritarianism*. Westwood, CT: Greenwood, 1982.

Holm, J. *Survey of Botswana Political Participation: Elite Survey*. Ann Arbor: Michigan, ICPSR, 1976.

Holm, J. and Molutsi, P. ed., *Democracy in Botswana*. Macmillan Botswana Publishing Company Ltd., 1989.

Hofferbert, Richard I. et al., *Parties, Policies, and Democracy*. Boulder: Westview Press, 1994.

Hyden, G., and Bratton M. ed., *Governance and Politics in Africa*. Boulder, 1992.

Huntington, S. P., *The Third Wave: Democratization in the Late Twentieth Century*. Norman: University of Oklahoma Press, 1991.

————. "How Countries Democratize." *Political Science Quarterly*, 1992 (106), pp. 579–616.

————. *Political Order in Changing Societies*. New Haven: Yale University Press, 1968.

————. "The Clash of Civilizations." *Foreign Affairs*. v. 72 (Summer 93).

*International Financial Statistics*. International Monetary Fund, Washington D.C., 1970, 1975, 185, 1990.

Inkeles A. *On Measuring Democracy: Its consequences and Concomitants*. New Brunswick, N.J., Transaction Publishers, 1991.

Ismagilova, R.N. *Ethnic Problems of the Tropical Africa, can they be solved?* Moscow: Progress Publishers, 1978.

Jackson, R. H., and Rosberg, C. G. "Democracy in in Tropical Africa." *Journal of International Affairs* 38, 2 (1985).

James, W., and Caliguire, D. "Renewing Civil Society." *Journal of Democracy*, vol. 7, No. 1, January 1996, 56–66.

Jeffries, R., "Rawlings and the Political Economy of Underdevelopment in Ghana." *African Affairs* 81, 384 (July 1982).

Karl, T. "Dilemmas of Democratization in Latin America." *Comparative Politics* 23, pp. 1–21.

Khama, S., Sir, *Botswana, A Developing Democracy in Southern Africa.* Uppsala: Scandinavian Institute of African Studies, 1970.

Lamberty, Y. *Ghana in Search of Stability, 1957–1992.* Westport, CT, Praeger 1993.

Lee, R., and Schlemmmer, L. ed., *Transition to Democracy: Policy Perspectives* 1991.

Lemarchand, R. "Africa's Troubled Transitions." *Journal of Democracy,* vol. 3, no. 4, October 1992.

Lerner, D. *The Passing of Traditional Society.* New York: Free Press, 1958.

Lijphart, A. *Democracy in Plural Societies.* New Haven: Yale University Press, 1977.

Linz J. J. "Church and State in Spain from the Civil War to the Return of Democracy." *Daedalus.* Vol. 120 (Summer 1991), pp. 159–78.

———. *Politics in Developing Countries: Comparing Experiences with Democracy.* Boulder, Colorado: L. Rienner Publishers 1990.

Linz, J. and Stepan, A. "Political Identities and Electoral Sequences: Spain, the Soviet Union, and Yugoslavia." *Daedalus.* pp. 121, 123–39, 1992.

Lipset, S.M. "Some Social Requisites of Democracy: Economic Development and Political Development." *American Political Science Review* 53, 1959, pp. 69–105.

———. *Political Man.* Baltimore: John Hopkins University Press, 1981.

———. *First New Nation.* New York: W. W. Norton, 1979.

———. "The Social Requisites of Democracy Revisited." *The American Sociological Review,* vol. 59 (Feb. 1994), pp. 1–24.

Londregan, J., Bienen, H., and Van De Walle, N. "Ethnicity and Leadership Succession in Africa." *International Studies Quarterly* (1995), 39, pp. 1–25.

Londregan, J., and Poole, K. "Poverty, The Coup Trap, and the Sei-zure of Executive Power." *World Politics.* Vol. 42 (January 1990), pp. 151–83.

Manning, A. R. *Mauritius: The Politics of Change.* Mayfield, East Sus-sex: Dodo Books, 1989.

Marsh, R. M. "Authoritarian and Democratic Transitions in National Political Systems." *International Journal of Comparative Soci-ology* XXX11, 3–4 (1991).

Massing, A. W. *Local Government Reform in Ghana: Democratic Re-newal or Autocratic Revival?* Verlug fur Entwicklungspolitik Breitenbach GmbH Saarbrucken, 1994.

Mazrui, Ali. A. *Cultural Forces in World Politics.* James Currrey Ltd, London, 1990.

————. *The Africans: A Triple Heritage.* London: BBC Publications, 1986.

————. *Soldiers and Kinsmen: The Making of a Military Ethnocracy.* Beverly Hills, Sage, 1975.

Mazrui, Ali A. and Tidy, Michael. *Nationalism and New States in Af-rica,* London: Heinemann Educational Books Ltd., 1984.

McColm, R. Bruce et al., *Freedom in the World, The Annual Survey of Political Rights and Civil Liberties,* 1980, 1990, 1992–93. New York: Freedom House, 1981, 1991, 1993.

McClintock, C. "The Prospects for Democratic Consolidation in a "Least Likely" case, Peru." *Comparative Politics,* Jan. 1989.

Mehta, Shiv Rattan. *Social Development in Mauritius: A Study on Ru-ral Modernization in an Island Community.* New Delhi: Wiley Eastern, 1981.

Michaels, M. "Retreat from Africa." *Foreign Affairs* 72, 1, 1993, pp. 93–108.

Morrison, D.G., Mitchell, R.C., and Paden J.N. *Understanding Black Africa.* Paragon House: New York 1989.

Mukela, J. *The IMF Fallout.* Africa Report, January–February 1987. pp. 65–67.

Munslow B. *Why has the Westminster Model fail in Africa?* Parlia-mentary Affairs. v. 36, 2, 1983.

Mwiinga, Jowie. *Chill for Chiluba,* Africa Report, vol. 39, (March/ April 1994), pp. 58–60.

Newbury, C. W. *British Policy Towards West Africa.* Oxford, Clarendon Press, 1965.

Nyerere, Julius K. *Freedom and Socialism. Uhuru na Ujamaa; A Selection from Writings and Speeches, 1965–1967.* Oxford University Press, 1968.

————. *Ujamaa—essays on socialism.* Oxford University Press, 1968.

Nyong'o, A. *Popular Struggles for Democracy in Africa.* London: Zed Books, 1987.

Nzongola-Ntalaja, G. *The African Crisis: The Way Out.* Sapes Books: Harare 1992.

O'Donnel, G. and Schmitter, P. *Transitions from Authoritarian Rule: Tentative Conclusions about Uncertain Democracy.* Baltimore, MD, John Hopkins University Press, 1986.

Pakulski, J. "Social Movements in Comparative Perspectives." in Louis Kriesberg and Bronislaw Misztal ed., *Research in Social Movements, Conflicts and Change.* Vol. 11, Greenwich, CT. 1988.

Panter-Brick, K. *Prospects for Democracy in Zambia, Government and Opposition.* 1992, pp. 231–47.

Picard, L. A. *The Politics of Development in Botswana: A model for Success?* Boulder: L. Rienner Publishers, 1987.

Pinkney, R. *Democracy in the Third World.* Boulder, Co: L. Rienner, 1994.

Pipes, D. *Friendly Tyrants: An American Dilemma.* New York: St. Martin's Press, 1991.

Pourgerami, A. *Development and Democracy in the Third World,* 1994.

Pridham, G. ed., *Encouraging Democracy: The International Context of Regime Transition in Southern Europe.* St. Martin's Press, NY, 1991.

Przeworski, A., Alvarez, M., Cheibub, J. A. and Limongi, F. "What Makes Democracy Endure." *Journal of Democracy,* vol. 7, Number 1, January 1996, pp. 39–55.

Przeworski, A. and Limongi, F. *Democracy and Development.* Paper Presented at the Nobel Symposium on Democracy. Uppsala, Sweden, 27–30 August, 1994.

Quainoo, S. E. *The Military Virus in the African Body-Politic.* Paper Presented at the 1994 New York African Studies Association, New Paltz.

Rothchild, D. ed. *The Political Economy of Recovery.* Lynne Rienner Publishers, Boulder 1991.

Rustow, D., and Erickson, K. P. ed. *Comparative Political Dynamics: Global Research Perspectives.* Harper Collins Publications, 1991.

————.*The Struggle for Nationhood, Modernization, and Leadership.* Washington D.C., Brookings Institution, 1967.

————. *Philosophers and Kings: Studies in Leadership.* New York, G. Braziller, 1970.

Sandbrook, R. *The Politics of Africa's Economic Recovery.* Cambridge University Press, 1993.

Share, D. "Transitions to Democracy and Transitions Through Transactions." *Comparative Political Studies,* vol. 19, No. 4, pp. 525–48.

————. *Transitions Through Transaction: The Politics of Democratization in Spain, 1975–1977,* Ph.D Dissertation. Stanford University.

Seong, K., Torres, J., and Lipset, S. M. "A Comparative Analysis of the Social Requisites of Democracy." *International Social Science Journal,* vol. 45, May 1993, pp. 155–75.

Schumpeter, J. *Capitalism, Socialism, and Democracy.* New York, Harper, 1950.

Simmons, A. S. *Modern Mauritius.* Indiana University Press, Bloomington, 1982.

Sklar, R. L. *Developmental Democracy,* Paper Delivered to the 1985 Annual Meeting of the American Political Science Association. New Orleans.

Sill, Mike." Sustaining a Success Story." *The Geographical Magazine,* vol. 65 (Feb. 1993), pp. 37–42.

Sommervile, Keith. "Botswana At The Crossroads." *The World Today,* vol. 50, (February 1994), pp. 22–24.

Stepan, A., and Skach, C. "Constitutional Framework and Democratic Consolidation: Parliamentarism versus Presidentialism." *World Politics,* vol. 46 (October 1993), pp. 1–22.

*The Christian Science Monitor.* April 23, 1996.

*The Constitution of the Republic of Ghana*. Ghana Publishing Corporation, 1992.

*The Daily Graphic*. January 10, 1990.

*The Economist*. November 20, 1993, p. 47.

*The Ghanaian Times*. November 6, 1991.

*The New Nations of West Africa*. 1990, p. 35.

———. 1960, p. 149.

*The New York Times*. January 3, 1988, p. 1.

The World Bank, *Sub-Saharan Africa, From Crisis to Sustainable Growth*. Washington D.C., 1989, xv.

*United Nations Development Program*. Human Development Report, 1980, 1985, 1990, 1994.

*United Nations Educational Scientific and Cultural Organization Report*. 1991.

Valentine, Theodore. "Mineral-led Economic Growth, Drought Relief, and Incomes Policy: Income Distribution in Botswana Reconsidered." *The American Journal of Economics and Sociology*, vol. 52 (Jan. 1993), pp. 31–49.

Vick, D. "Democratic Tide Turns Africa Towards a New Economic Era." *Africa Business*, January 1992, pp. 10–13.

Weiner, M. Political Change: Asia, Africa, and the Middle East, in Weiner and Huntington, *Understanding Political Development* 38. Durham, N.C.: Duke University Press, 1987

*West Africa*. 26 February–March 3, 1996, pp. 309–12

Widner, J. ed., *Political Reform in Anglophone and Francophone African Countries in Economic Change and Political Liberalization in Sub-Saharan Africa*. John Hopkins University Press, 1994, pp. 49–79.

Zaffiro, James J. "Mass Media, Politics and Society in Botswana: the 1990s and Beyond." *Africa Today*, vol. 40, No. 1 (1993), pp. 7–25.

Zhang, B. "Corporatism, Totalitarianism, and Transitions to Democracy." *Comparative Political Studies*, vol. 27, No. 1, April, 1994, 108–36.